IF LOVE CORRUPTS, DOES ABSOLUTE LOVE CORRUPT ABSOLUTELY?

TONY: What is this game I am playing, this throwback to our days of pure erotica? I play SM games out of Kraft-Ebing. I know way back in my corrupt brain what I'm doing, and I know why I'm doing it . . .

KATE: Tony Amato owns me. I must do his will! He is enjoying his power. If I am coming apart Christa doesn't notice. I am a model mother. I am here when my husband comes home for dinner. I hold my lover in my arms, I tell him I love him in my head. I am without shame, morals, or common sense . . .

AFFAIR

Antony Amato &
Katherine Edwards

BALLANTINE BOOKS • NEW YORK

Library of Congress Catalog Card Number: 77-20490

ISBN: 0-345-27998-0

This edition published by arrangement with G. P. Putnam's Sons

Manufactured in the United States of America

First Ballantine Books Edition: March 1979

Author's Note

BY

ANTONY AMATO

When I was nine, my father let me have a morocco-bound datebook that he had received as a Christmas gift from a business associate. I immediately inscribed it with my name and then, on January 4, 1948, began my career as a diarist with the entry: "I hate Mrs. Rupert. I kissed Debbie Smith 3 times outside."

I have been keeping track of such personal information in various-sized notebooks for almost thirty years now, including those six months in 1973 and '74 when I was overwhelmingly in love with the woman who is called, here, Katherine Edwards.

Katherine insists that I am the one who thought of publishing our diaries of that period. I recollect that she came up with the idea first, although only as a joke. It does not really matter. I doubt whether either of us would have done it alone. Even though we are both writers and therefore have, from time to time, found ideas for stories in our respective diaries, I don't think either of us ever expected to expose our lives quite so nakedly as we do here.

Here is how I recall it came about:

Sometime in March of '74, not long after Kate and I had become lovers, we each discovered that the other kept a diary. At the time, this seemed like one more miraculous similarity that bound us together. It also seemed as if our ultimate act of intimacy would be to show each other our diaries. It took us weeks before we had the courage to do this, and when we did—

nude, in front of the fire on an early April after-noon—we were sure that we had crossed a final threshold in our relationship. Perhaps we had.

By the time Kate and I reached that afternoon of naked diary reading, the writing project which had originally brought us together—a heavily researched novel based on the Rockefeller family—was already grinding to a halt. And one of us (I do think it was Kate) said, "Hell, let's publish these instead. It's better than the Rockefellers any day." That line, "It's better than the Rockefellers any day," became a sort of running gag for us right up to the end.

One year later I was sitting alone in my apartment in Amsterdam trying to write a story about the affair we had had. I leafed through my diary and, reading about Kate and me in front of the fire, I thought: The story is here and in Kate's diary. It is already written and it's better than the Rockefellers any day. It had been over seven months since Kate and I had been in contact when I wrote to her, proposing that we really do publish the diaries of our affair. Her answer arrived a few weeks later in a small box; she sent me a typed manuscript of her diary and some notes on how to disguise our identities. She asked me to take care of the editing and sale of the manuscript myself.

I did. And I now offer it to the reader with a mix-ture of embarrassment, exhilaration, and utter amaze-ment.

Part I

Sunday nights are different from Sundays. Almost holy. The hot bath. Mingus. *The Times*. The late movie. Maybe even a Sunday night screw???

I love Sunday nights. Plus I think I've finally thought of an idea for a book that will make money. Big real money. Will call Edith. (Does talking to your diary mean you're schizo?)

Sunday night blessings: heavy sound of Chris's breathing from next room—Rolf's corduroy ass against my bathrobe. (Meaningful pressure?) My own clean, baby-oiled elbows, wet, steamy hair around my neck, Q-tipped ears. Nothing I simply MUST read in the magazine section. Just *Bad Day at Black Rock* coming up—Rolf and me.

I keep the tips of my fingers under Rolf's weight, flipping the first and second sections, before showtime. I feel the pillow under my back in not quite the right place, only don't move it because maturity has taught me that there is no right place. I wonder about the signals from Rolf's ass.

The window is closed. Outside the air is cold and clean. I can smell Aunt Concetta's clean sheets flapping in my memory, and then I feel it. Rolf's hand. The sound of his "Mmmmmmmmm." I was right. Less than twenty minutes to showtime, but get rid of Concetta's sheets, and get ready. He runs the back of his hand against my breasts without feeling anything through the quilted robe. That's what I wanted, didn't

3

I, giving him the lean and hungry look all day? . . .
Well, then, shape up! And unwrap, only nineteen
minutes till the title and credits. A nineteen-minute,
Sunday night curtain raiser. Unless I'd rather put it off
till tomorrow, his eyes ask.

· I'd rather not. Tomorrow has a way of melting over
the weeks like lukewarm fudge, as he groans throatily
and parts my V. Okay, it's only sound effects, but I
groan back. He reaches—I revolve—a licking
sound—a loving it. Sunday Nights are as ritualized as
eleven o'clock Mass as I smell his saliva smear the
breast that has just found his hand. I also feel his ca-
blestitching irritate my nudity.

He slides off the bed. He wrestles with the other side
of my bikinis, raking them off my ankle, and checking
his Omega at the same time. You beast, I giggle to myself, stroking his ear with my woodpecker tongue, you
and I have come this come how many Sunday Nights
before? Don't you think I know your tricks? Responding by the numbers—his—knowing exactly which
Push/Pull will result in which Pulsing Prize: One sta-
men inserted into one pistil equals one whistle per
Cracker Jacks box per customer, but if you're greedy
and cheat against a hand, a tongue, a moment, there's
always a quick extra. . . .

The "time frame" for foreplay has been played out.
I must go to install the Margaret Sanger shield to the
sounds of running water. . . . It seems to me I've
heard this song before. I stare at myself in the mirror,
opening the robe to peek at myself. Rolf's big fat
plunger points at me through the bathroom wall. All
swollen and shiny. I go back to collect my innings.

Both our eyes closed. Both making throaty grunts.
Both concentrating elsewhere (me, wondering what
he's seeing on the inside of those lids and why it is we
don't stare into our wet retinas anymore, old Ravel afternoons that lasted till way past Spencer Tracy). My
legs wrapped around him up high. The thick,

bunched-up soft bathrobe still partly between us,
middle to middle. The shut-eyed knowledge of each
other's flesh as familiar as the breakfast table. He's
holding back—not yet, not yet, a couple more minutes.
It's true—we know each other a million times better
than the breakfast table; his finger up me, his fingers
squeezing me, his tongue, his cock, until there I go,
over the hilt. There I go. . . . Sundays are never
strawberries in January, but over just the same. This
distinctive moment is as close to suicide as we come
these days. Me 'n' him, my old friend, whose body I
know the same as my own, a mole back there under
his wing, a familiar loggy weight that's nicer than belly
mink.

"More," I swallow, squeezing with my thighs. "Not
yet; the hell with Robert Ryan." Only it's over. The
pain's gone, isn't it? That gnawing toothache pain.
"Didn't I hear that roller-coaster cry you give out, that
banshee bellow of yours? Don't be a hog, woman,
that's enough for one Sunday Night; you goin' Forty-
second Street on me?"

"Not me," I tell him, "sure." And anything else he
wants to hear as he slaps my ass till it stings, and then
gets up for a quick trip to the fridge and maybe a pee
before *Black Rock*. The blue light, sound down, glowing in the distance. The sleeping sound of the child
through the walls. The *Fashions of The Times*. It's
nice, All of it. Even the come-hither crook of my unfinished snatcheroo. That's nice, too, it goes with the
feel of his hand on my foot as Spencer Tracy takes on
the whole damn town with one arm behind his back.

(On the bus up from New York)

After a visit with Ted amidst his scrambled family, I was in the mood for something neat, something sunnyside up. Over the course of the whole weekend, Ted and I only managed to stitch together a single conversation of the kind we used to throw off in a half hour over dinner at college. He left me at the airport half-apologetic/half-defensive; the defensive part seemed to say, "Hey, pal, *you're* the one who hasn't grown up."

True enough, Ted, and to prove your point, I immediately saunter off in the direction of a pair of smartly tailored, yolk-yellow slacks I see disappearing into a news shop. This is not my prolonged adolescence, Ted, old pal, it is my *delayed* adolescence. I am finally getting in my thirties what I only wet-dreamed of in my teens.

Yolk-yellow is buying the last copy of *The New Yorker* in Portland, Maine.

"Don't you have any more of those left?" I ask the mag man.

He says, "No," and starts to explain how he usually has too many left over on Sundays, but in a twinkle I am saying to Yellow Bottom, "Then I'm afraid you'll have to share that one with me on the plane."

"I beg your pardon?" she says.

"I can't wait to get back to New York either," I say, sending off a conspiratorial smile.

And, yes, I've done it again. In a split second I have detected that critical vanity which will allow my prick to get warm and wet deep in the night. Yes, indeed, Yellow Bottom finds these weekend jaunts to the backwoods of her childhood excruciating. If only Moms didn't dote on her visits so. Yes, the pines are gorgeous, but, oh, the boredom of it all. How ya gonna keep 'em down on the farm after they've seen Daly's Dandelion? I keep under wraps that I live in the woods myself, best to work up to that through a discussion of health foods (which I get to somewhere over Providence).

A word about sexual congress: Would I ever have thought up this complicated business on my own? If I had been born into *rarum naturum* amongst a bunch of grunting bipeds, would I have thought of sticking my thing in there? In that out-of-the-way crevice with all its cul-de-sacs? Wouldn't I have found her armpit more convenient? Or her ear? Wouldn't I have tried her belly button first? Or certainly her ass? (Fact is, I did try Yellow Bottom's ass.) And would I have thought of putting my elbows here, knees there, and thumping around like this? I'm sure not. Even with the help of Dr. Greenspan's *Sexual Happiness for All,* I didn't get it right for months in my college days. I remember working away at Lucy in Adams' House, the head of my poor dick smacking against the sheets with each thrust as it skimmed through her slit perpendicularly (that's what it looked like you were supposed to do, according to Greenspan's illustrations!). No, sir, if I had been Picanthropus Erectus, the Amato line would have ended with me. Evolution does not spring from an armpit.

It doesn't spring from a diaphragm either, which Yellow (Betty) Bottom had been wearing all the way from Maine. I wonder what she and Moms have going there.

Oh, yes, Diary, if you must know, I fucked her. I fucked her with a practiced fuck. I added one more to the Gross National Fuck.

Then, why, you may ask, why do I feel so lonely this morning?

Just got back from New York. Saw Edith. Can an agent be senile at thirty-five? She's turned my little idea into a thousand-page Rockefeller tome, a full-blooded, fully researched biographical history. Me? Doesn't she read any of the ten percent of my work that clothes her? Irving Wallace, Edie-an industry with catacombs filled with busy little researchers, cross-indexers—he writes thousand-page histories. I am a deep, serious, even contemplative thinker, Edie. Okay, a cookbook every now and then, but the entire panoramic putsch from John D. to the Shah of Exxon? The woman has lost her grip.

I decide to call Minckoff to go partners. Reporters have logical, concise minds. Helpful. Besides . . . Minckoff's cute. (Cute?) I thought Minckoff was married and faithful.

QUESTION: Is your old friend Minckoff faithful?

ANSWER: What the hell do you care?

NOTE: (FRIENDLY OBSESSION): Here we go again. Will I ever think of anything but sex, sex, sex? All of us. Dorcas just called. This time she's hot after the kid's gym teacher. And Angie, with her D'Agostino delivery boy, and before D'Agostino's, what about the guy who came to give them an estimate on their septic field in Copake? (What is it with us happily marrieds? Or do all married women play with their septic field hands?) Even Liz, who reads *Family Circle,* drove all the way to Hastings, deliberately speeding so a state policeman would stop her by the side of the road.

Times, they are beginning to scare me, moving on as they are, with us caught midway between the panty girdle and missed chances. . . . Or is there estrogen enough in the old bag yet? Angie? Angie Lagamazio Boutis, oldest of old friends, you tell me? What do you think is in store for us? Angie, you are me, a woman facing the doldrums of her life . . . condemned to watching her own daughter stuff six pounds of loose boobs into her ripped T-shirts. . . . Tell me, Angie, do the delivery boys of this world really want a piece of our ripened pulchritude?

Dorcas, Liz, Me: we're all of us obsessed. We, us, are fast turning into women of "a certain age. . . ." And it stinks!

NOTE: (FRIENDLY OBSESSION): Rolf says I'm going through a waning powers panic. And that I'm over-compensating. And that I'm a nympho. (At Once?) Anyway, he's smelled something and turned it into an ultimate weapon. Quite a strategic advantage, knowing that two days off his flinty dole and I'm a slavering junkie, *who'll do anything for a fix!*

Or: Could it be he is NOT a nympho? (Consider the stereophonic sex of yesteryear with yesterday's Victor Red Seal go-round.)

No: It's a weapon. If I make him mad, he won't. Never was one to scatter his seeds out of context . . . whereas me? A woman of a certain age. Would she hump Horton the Elephant on a blind date?

ANTONY
September 20

A long day at the window watching the geese form up for their trip to the Carolinas. Virgil tells me geese live to over a hundred, that the same gaggle has spent the summers on his pond for four generations of his family. I mentioned to him that that meant these very geese were commuting to the South during the Civil War, which struck me as an ironic thought. It didn't strike Virgil one way or the other. If I married a local girl and settled down, Virgil would still think the geese belonged here more than I. Maybe he's right. While these geese were vacationing in the Confederacy, my folks were mending harnesses in Naples.

Staring at geese is not conducive to clever CBS "Afternoon Playhouse" thoughts. I have to produce five story outlines by Tuesday next to be in the running. I keep coming up with dopey, sentimental ones, like: Young man discovers he has leukemia and does not want to die without having children, so he proposes to his neighbor who is deaf. Actually, there's probably a great symbolic tale in there somewhere which those fools at CBS will fail to understand. I can hear them now: "Not bad, Amato, but we're kind of loaded up with leukemia at the moment, don't you know?" How about leprosy? Or maybe terminal consciousness?

Annamarie has promised to bring me dinner tonight, something neat and clean in a Danish casserole dish, no doubt, and then, with my lips still dripping from white wine sauce, I will bury my tongue in her muff, her gingham skirt over my head like a cheerful circus tent. I am nothing if not accommodating. Annamarie likes to have as much out of sight as possible during my little forays. It allows her to focus without distraction as I slobber away on her privates. And how scrubbed and sweet her privates are. When God made Nordic women, he dabbed honey in their vaginal ducts.

Yes, a long day—from geese to ducts.

KATHERINE
October 12

If Rolf doesn't do me tonight, by tomorrow it'll be two weeks. If his cock isn't in a sling it ought to be. (Does that make any sense?)

ANTONY
October 14

What is wrong with me?

One life, Tony, old boy. One. Get it? This is not a rehearsal. This is it. This minute is it.

When did I get it into my head that "getting by" was some kind of an achievement?

Snakes get by.

Look at yourself. You're a goddamned adolescent. Good Christ, so you fuck women. You've turned it into a fucking game of tag. Look at all the goddamned energy you invest in that pitiful ten seconds of squirting.

Jesus God, didn't I have more in mind ten years ago? More than this fucking genital census count? More than this mindless afternoon TV plotting?

Oh, please, there has to be more. I don't care if I'm not an artist, but I want something more than this skimming life of mine. We should have stayed in Naples. There would be more substance to my life working in the Fiat factoria than this.

Shit, I'm lonely.

I had some—what?—depth? soul? vision?—back then, didn't I? What happens to it? Does it grow over, like a wound? I refuse to go to bed until I feel something.

Anything more than an itch.

KATHERINE
October 14

Angela doesn't think I'm crazy. The truth is I think maybe Sam's going through the same sort of doldrum

11

as Rolf. But why don't they want to? Is that normal?
God help me, for three hours last night I drove
through the night screaming, I want a lover, I want a
lover!!! I thought it was men who were always after
it—I want a lover? Me, am I going out of my mind? I
am in love with my husband and always have been. I
love my husband. Believe me, I love him.

Then why did I get in the car at twelve and stay in it
until a quarter to three screaming so loud I lost my
voice.

A lover?

No, Rolf's right, what I need is to get into the
Rockefeller book. Good idea! Why haven't you called
Minckoff? Call Minckoff!

But why not a lover? All it is is unused energy. Ask
Reich. What the hell am I supposed to do with it and
don't tell me typing'll take it away. I know what'll take
it away.

Two weeks and four days exactly.

ANTONY
October 15

Still got the "what's-it-all-about?" blues.

For solace, reading Van Gogh's letters and Goethe's
notebooks. Oh, God, what I'd do for an ounce of their
passion.

But then again, I came across this note from
Goethe:

"Like everything which is not the involuntary result
of fleeting emotion but the creation of time and will,
any marriage, happy or unhappy, is infinitely more
interesting and significant than any romance, however
passionate."

That one gave me a curious feeling. He must have
known something I don't.

KATHERINE
October 15

I think I understand. I mean, I know I understand,
except I'm not sure it'll help. Rolf says our sex for him
is just like his subscription to *Art in America*. He used
to have a subscription. He doesn't anymore. Recently
he's been thinking of resubscribing. Why make such a
big deal about it? Or, "Maybe," he says, as if he is
mentioning when asparagus will be in season, "maybe
you just don't turn me on these days. Ever think of
that?"

The truth is, I hadn't. No, that thought had not occurred to me. But for one minute it made me feel better about my having driven around for three solid
hours last night screaming into the windshield. And
why should it?

ANTONY
October 18

Down to the city to finish off my CBS treatment
with Leonard's help. New York is an oasis of vicious
reality after too much of the dreary Currier & Ives
landscape I now call home. In the country, I begin to
feel like Henry Miller on his trip to Liechtenstein: I
long for a single delinquent face: I crave the armpit
stench of desperate humanity, a wordless, faceless,
thigh-to-thigh encounter with a fellow subway rider.
But my two enemies, Boredom and Despair, have split
ranks and are trying a pincer on me. Boredom lives in
the country, Despair in the city. My only moments of
hopefulness are on the bus between the two—going in

either direction, for that matter. I thrive on contrasts. Wherever I am, the oasis is thataway.

Leonard is a wonderful help to me, broadens my characters and sharpens my plots to make them "television real." The more successful he becomes, the more generous he is, and I think I am finally ready truly to admire him. "Work is salvation," he tells me. It's wonderful: We Catholics need Jews to teach us Calvinism. I'm trying. I want very much to sell the script to CBS. If all goes well, I'll take the royalties and treat myself to a couple of months in Scandinavia. Ice-blue lakes, blond beaches.

While Leo and I are working on my treatment, a friend of Sally's calls. She needs a place to stay for the night and since Leo is due at Sally's later, can she sleep at his place? Leo informs her that I will be sleeping there, but that she can use the other bed if neither of us minds.

This woman, Marion, an athletic-looking blonde, arrives a few hours later, shakes hands with both of us, takes a shower, and plunges into bed with her T. S. Eliot. Leo and I barely look at her as we put wrinkles in my plot (about a geriatric romance), and by the time Leo leaves, Marion is asleep. I take a closer look at her all curled up in Leo's bathrobe. Marion seems to be a pretty girl.

I work another two hours on the treatment, only moderately distracted by the fact of an athletic blonde lying (now with her knees up) only ten feet from my typewriter. Then pull out the convertible bed, undress, close my eyes, sigh, and proceed to become obsessed by Marion. I cough. Open and close the window a few times, my swollen pecker only two feet away from her sleep-pouted mouth as I sashay back and forth. I decide simply to crawl into her bed and screw her without saying a word, hoping she will take it as part of a dream. I decide against it. I smoke. I send her erotic thought messages; "Wake up, Marion. Fuck me,

Marion." I have no idea why I am so obsessed. I wasn't particularly randy when I arrived in the city. Marion is attractive, yet hardly a knockout. But it becomes a moral issue: Marion and I are wasting a unique opportunity. It would be unholy to pass it up. I don't remember having a sexual obsession like this since my teens. I don't think I fell asleep until nearly five, and then I promptly had a dream in which Leo and Sally are taking Marion and me on a train ride to Philadelphia. I assualt Marion, standing up in a passageway, and I come before her pants are down. I believe this was my first wet dream in over a year and, waking up, I realize that it was clearly my best orgasm in memory. I feel marvelous, higher than a kite, and then Marion wakes up. She goes to the bathroom without looking at me. When she returns, still in Leo's robe, I am sitting up in bed, smoking.

I say, "I just had the best sexual experience of my life, with you."

She grins and says, "Me, too."

"I mean it," I say. "I had a wet dream that came straight from my spinal column."

"I mean it, too," she says. "I dreamt about you and you were marvelous."

She then proceeds to shed the robe and pull on her underwear. I invite her to come sit with me in bed, but she declines, saying she doesn't want to ruin our relationship. A few minutes later she leaves, throwing me a kiss from the doorway and promising to return that evening. She never did. Leo and Sally chose last night to fight, so I am spending tonight with Leo, typing and comforting.

I believe my relationship with Marion is the best I've ever had.

KATHERINE
October 19

WHAT I NEED: To take my typewriter into a cold shower with me.

WHAT I WANT: To stay the closed-shop woman I've always been. Keeping the freckles on the insides of my thighs known only to those who already know and have long since forgotten, except Rolf, who says on accounta them he'd always be able to identify me in a crowd. Jimmy Stewart is not as tall as my husband, his middle toe not as long. Does Jimmy Stewart wear 12B? Aha, I thought not. Yellow-haired fingers and tiny Dracula teeth. Neither does Jimmy Stewart look like the discus thrower naked.

ANTONY
October 19

Handed in my CBS treatment. Leo thinks it's fine.

Then out for an evening which lasted the whole night with Saskia, the Dutch journalist I met at Doug's a few weeks back. Saskia is twenty-one going on forty, lusty and impersonal in the grand Nordic tradition, and smart as a whip. I like her very much, but for most of the evening (going from club to club with Joe and Willie after Joe's play) she seemed to have little interest in me. Toward 1:00 A.M., I touched her hand tentatively and she pressed it against her bosom and smiled, looking me straight in the eye for the first time that night. We petted like sophomores (sophomores of my era) for the rest of the night, having no place to go. I loved it. My two days in the city have provided

me with my happiest sexual encounters in some time,
neither of them involving naked screwing. I think I feel
a wave of puritanism coming on, or at least a period
when a stolen kiss means more than a free fuck. Willie
reports the same. He has spent two consecutive Saturday nights sleeping fully clothed under Joe's piano with
a lady named Iris. He says it is terrific; he wants to
bring back bundling. I can see it overtaking the country by storm: bundling and dry humping, touching
breasts outside sweaters, quick hickies in darkened
hallways.

KATHERINE
October 21

"Come on over," Minckoff says, "we'll see." Except
when I get there the pounding in my wrists echoes
through the room. How come?, I wanna know, you
and Minckoff have been alone a million times with no
such echoes. *Except the pounding in his wrists isn't so
quiet either* (as he tells me) shrugging, "I don't know
... all your Rockefellers; it's a big job."

He reaches across me for a Camel.

I continue to wonder (because of driving through
the night wanting something I never wanted before?).
We continue talking Rockefeller. I tell him what I told
Edith. How Rocky's going to run for the BIG Office,
how it's a guaranteed, surefire prepresidential shoo-
in—a book on the candidate no matter who wins. I can
feel the hairs on Fred Minckoff's arm bristling.
Freddie? I've always been the wife of his friend, a pro-
tected species. How come today his breath is as loud as
a semitruck up a very high hill? Rockefeller, Freddie,
talk to me of Rockefeller . . . just before he lunges.

Minckoff? Lunging at me? Have I changed my
scent? from Lanvin to Lascivious? And that's when I

heard myself shouting and pushing him off. No, that is definitely not the right scenario, Freddie. Get your hands off my measled thighs. Under contract to Rolf. Remember Rolf?

"Stop it, Freddie," who doesn't; why can't he understand it's only the idea of him, or of somebody who doesn't have the slightest resemblance?

There is safety in longing.

Beware the twenty-two-year-old bearing Gym lessons.

Why isn't Fred Minckoff listening to me as I look down and read "Que Pasa" upside down on my underpants, in green and red embroidery, "Que Pasa" undies in a stranger's fingers.

Que pasa avec Fred Minckoff?

I will hurt you if you don't stop. Please don't hurt me, Freddie. Freddie, you're the kind of guy you slap on the back like Pat O'Brien used to slap good old Ronnie Reagan, why are you listening in on the wrong wavelengths?

We must speak of Nelson Rockefeller and tea with milk, no sugar, no lemon.

I must go home and telephone Angie, Dorcas, and Liz. I will tell them.

Fantasies are not for fulfilling. At least driving through the evening screaming is familiar and needs no further instructions.

KATHERINE
October 22

THE AFTERMATH: Otherwise referred to as The Old Hankering—It Hankers On. Or—Regardless of Minckoff!

As for calling the girls, one lesson in thigh-grabbing doesn't necessarily tell the whole story. Because why did I dream last night of a banquet? A stuffing, gorging, slobbering, wallowing kind of banquet where everywhere pieces of fat asses and stuffed pigs smelled good enough to eat? In which the lesson was:

Fish or cut bait

Who am I to teach moral lessons? Guilt lies in the coveting. *And I still covet, I swear to God; I woke up sweating, coveting like crazy!*

ANTONY
October 24

After a long, drunken supper, Willie and I decided that what is missing from our lives is the soft boredom of domesticity. We shed real tears yearning for the bliss of tedious married life.

Willie: I'm tired of hard-edged fucks. I want a good, old habitual fuck. You know, a it's-Saturday-night-and-we-haven't-done-it-in-a-week fuck.

Me: Christ, yes. The kind where you don't get a hard-on until the very last moment.

Willie: Exactly.

Me: Or better yet, the kind you try to get out of. I remember trying to put Bonnie asleep with long stories, hoping she'd forget about it.

Willie: Right, but you don't get out of it, so you end up having a soft, sleepy fuck, and as soon as it's over you think, Thank God that's out of the way.

From there, we go into fits of nostalgia for damp brassieres hanging from the shower curtain and piles of Tampax under the sink.

Willie: You just can't get these things from a one-night stand.

And so we plan a series of Domestic Weekends. The

idea is to find the most wifeish partners we can dig up (preferably divorcées) and to schedule two full days of dreariness with them instead of our usual bon vivant, nonstop weekend parties. Willie and I were up until four listing the activities.

Friday night: TV turkey dinners (with apple juice) while watching "Jeopardy." No fire, no candles, no incense, and especially no wine or pot. Fall asleep on couch during "Starlight Movie."

Saturday morning: Up early, coffee and sunny-side ups, followed by grocery and hardware shopping in Kingston. Buy beer and cigarettes.

Saturday afternoon: Watch "Wide World of Sports," handholding only.

Saturday night: Scrabble and Hamburger Helper. A quickie at the very last moment.

Sunday morning: Up early to clean oil burner.

We have not planned a weekend so eagerly for months.

KATHERINE
October 23

I cannot bring myself to look at myself in the mirror bought and paid for by my husband who would think my moral dissolution unthinkable in me, his wife, for whom he has sacrificed his Art. Given his all.

I must remember he could have lived in a garret alone, you know. It's part of the job. I must be grateful. And yet—

I am ungrateful, low-down, rotten, and without a vestige of gratitude. And truly and honestly do not want to want what I seem to! To be young and sated and weightless and grateful and still want what they want in *Seventeen* magazine. That's what I want.

Then how come I don't?
Then how come I'm not?

Ho, hee! The best-laid-plans department.

Pursuant to Plan A, heretofore known as Domestic Weekend #1, Willie and I added sixty-eight message units to our phone bill Wednesday in search of the perfect weekend wife. Willie came up with one lulu named (no kidding) Lulu, a Bensonhurst divorcée who used to take piano lessons from him in his tamer days. She said she'd be thrilled.

"Don't be thrilled," Willie said, winking to me. "We'll just have a quiet weekend around the house."

And I dug deep, coming up with Cindy Albert, a throwback to my own days of domesticity in the Heights. Cindy was a neighbor then and spent the night of the Blackout with Bonnie and me talking about pastries. I told her we were having kind of a bake-in up here and wouldn't she like to come with a few cupcake tins? She would.

They arrived together on the 6:15 bus ("It gave us a chance to get acquainted before we had to deal with you lugs."—Lulu. Lugs! Perfect casting, Willie, old boy), and then came back to the house all giggles.

"I'll get dinner ready," says Willie, poking around in the freezer for the Swanson's, and with that Bensonhurst and Cindy whip upstairs to freshen themselves.

A few minutes and I yell up, "Hey, Cindy, did you remember the cupcake tins?"

"Yup," she calls, and then trips down the stairs in scoops of pure chiffon.

Willie doubles over. "Is that your baking outfit?"

"Nope," she sighs, "just the cupcakes."

And so it went.

Little Lulu's housedress was even more to the point

and along with it she had a bottle of tequila (Willie's oldest weakness) dangling from her fingertips.

We never made it to "Starlight Movie."

Why don't women ever take me seriously?

KATHERINE
November 2

Minckoff won't do book. (It serves me right.) Have to keep telling myself, it's okay, over and over, it's okay, *you didn't. You didn't.* You are still one hundred percent—a Good Wife. What you're supposed to be.

Except it still serves me right, too.

Guilt lies in the coveting, sans doute.

KATHERINE
November 3

Rolf snores loud on his back, less loud on his side, very low on his stomach. But he always snores. (Repressed asthma?)

2:00. I'm awake.

For some reason I suddenly know that if it's two here it's eleven at Bakersfield, California. I got up for a pickle and a slice of Jarlsberg, except I went instead to the phone and called (I am embarrassed to say) Buck Blackman, who, after fifteen years, I'm sure was still to be found behind a lobster trap, up to his ass in seaweed, in that never-never past I so wanted to share with him, through sickness and ennui. Am I really calling that Buck Blackman, who thinks poetry comes in Hallmark cards? Who used to "feed his face" and probably still does? Who used to spend Saturday afternoon underneath the guts of his black Plymouth on a regular basis? Who, to give him credit, had the good sense not to carry me off to the Moby Dick country where, he must have known, after I finally had my fill of him, I'd have rotted on his clam hook or come asunder . . . and him with it?

So I couldn't understand why. Why I bothered to trace him through an old alumni annual and find out the area code. Listening to the slightly childish drawl that was that many light-years away from me.

"I looked for you at the reunion," he told me. "Did you see *The Way We Were?* Gee, I thought of us. Where are you? You know I still have all your pictures?"

"No kidding," I said, but even with my eyes closed there wasn't any image to connect with. The operator told me that's who he was—the very same name out of my paths-not-taken. But all the wires were too crossed anyway.

"Remember Wimpy? The guy I bought the motorcycle from? And what about old Stretch, I see him every once in a couple years. Old Stretch never got on so good with women, you know. . . . Remember when we went canoeing, Stretch and that girl?"

Only, the thing was I didn't remember any of it. Not the show, the motorcycle or old Stretch. Just my tears. Riding away from Rochester on a Greyhound bus without him. They tasted exactly like the ones I'm still eating. While I stood there with the receiver in my hand like a jackass. With nothing to say because who was there on the other end to say it to?

One down and how many to go?

That was the part that scared me. If I called Buck Blackman on the phone at two o'clock in the morning, what else might I do? And why was I doing it?

And was there aspirin I could take for it?

And Rolf?

And Christa?

And why, after all these years, did only the tears taste familiar?

PROJECT FOR WEEK: Know thyself, you bitch. Call Dr. B. It's time for a refresher course in headhunting.

KATHERINE
November 8

Fought with Rolf again last night. Six days, six fights. Never about anything. Not true . . . but how do you fight about *that???????????* The *that* that is. *Rolf's fault . . . yes, your fault. . . . If you'd do me like you used to do, I wouldn't always be foaming at the fore the way I am. Rolf's fault. . . . Rolf's fault. . . . Rolf's fault.*

My husband has a woman who comes to him softly, Gently Johnny, she holds his golden head and sings to him over her dulcimer. How quietly he undresses her, how soft is her body. Come home, Gently Johnny, don't you think I know the words, too?

Does he? the SOB? Where the hell is he?

ANTONY
December 20

I have a weakness for Nazis. It probably comes from being taken for a Jew most of my life. Bonnie used to say Italians were God's dumb Jews. Every day I remember some remark of Bonnie's like that. Six years and I'm still trying to convince myself it was really difficult to love that woman. It really was, Tony, old boy. You sure are a hell of a slow learner.

As one of God's dumb Jews, I find Nazis stimulating. Invigorating. Always good for a game of

Scratch-the-Romantic-and-Find-the-Fascist. A fine Nazi woman is a jump in the ice-blue lake after a sauna. After five years in the sauna with Bonnie, I continue to crave Teutons. Got *Fräulein-wunder*. And what should appear at the Prestons' dinner party but the genuine article: Helga. Straight blond hair worn like a helmet with tassels. Not tassels, whips. Eyes the color of Aqua Velva. Tall, tight-skinned, smooth. And healthy, healthy, healthy. I imagine those Aryan legs wrapped around my middle and I immediately feel tubercular. I always work by contrasts. Next to Bonnie I felt healthy.

Helga has me thinking about Gerda and Gerda about Bonnie. Just how the hell long ago was it? When did the Year of the Soft Prick end?

I've just looked back at volume six of this thing. It was six and a half years ago. My handwriting was wilder. Oh, Jesus, I feel peculiar now. I've turned into such a fucking fraud. Such a fucking, little, tough-guy fraud. My erstwhile impotence was my last vestige of innocence. *Impotence has been maligned.* I couldn't get it up because in my heart of hearts I knew I didn't love my wife. My prick had honesty in those days. Conscience, not guilt. Something the shrinks wouldn't know about. Oh, but you'd be proud of me today, Doctor. Gerda straightened me out for good. I'm hard now. I fuck mud. If it asks.

Now Gerda, there was a real sentimentalist. She whimpered when I told her that in Spain I had dined for months on pussycat stew. "How could you?" I told her that I had thought it was bunny rabbit stew. She called me a pig and then proceeded to encourage me to fuck her, which I did with dispatch and finesse and piglike grunts. Gerda was my live-in tutorial in German Romanticism. She made me a man. My capsule lesson in vaginal fascism. How quickly her whimpering over digested pussycats made my pecker rifle hard. Sylvia

Plath said, "All women adore a fascist." Correct. And
we *become* fascists so someone will adore us. Most of
us would have never thought of it on our own. Born
under different circumstances, I would have been an SS
guard with a weepy wife.

   I am out of cigarettes, so think I will turn in.

   I doubt if I will call Helga.

   NOTE: One kindred spirit at the Prestons', a spider
lady named Katherine, an unladylike novelist (heard of
her, never read her) who wanted to pick my brain
about TV writing. A real wop hustler like my sister-
in-law. Married and horny. "Married and Horny,"
sounds like the title for a new feminist pop song.

   Good night.

KATHERINE
December 20

   Dinner at Prestons'.

   A friend of Lolly's from the city. Antony somebody.
Now lives here. Looks like me (Think Pacino, Hell's
Kitchen). The skinny wop with arms too long for his
body. Wrote some TV something.

   A German/Swedish *Fräulein* (Olga? Brunhilda?).
Blond pubic hair. Stupid. Her PR, productions . . .
something-shoddy husband in madras shirt. Hair pushing out his nostrils. She's on the make. All over the
wop from TV.

   Yacof and Nina. (If one more person tells me how
smart he is!) His voice never off middle C. "Yah, vell,
I am a neoeclectic, neo-Eriksonian, neo-I'm Okay,
You're in Trouble, joost listen, vile I interpolate you
under the table. . . ."

   Left early. Always. Rolf doesn't like parties. Doesn't
like small talk. Doesn't like anything that doesn't have
to do with art, struggle, value, work, the nature of ten-

sion (see Diary 1964, 1965, 1966, 1967, 1968, 1969—etc.) or the picture plane.

What about Intimate Art? he wants to know. He wraps a farmer's cows in 103 rolls of toilet paper, they beat it into the dung, only the farmer and he know about it. What if he climbs the back side of the Flatiron Building and sticks out his tongue at the typing pool? Then he's gone, was he ever there? This is Art, he says, art doesn't mirror life, it makes it happen. Covers the rough spots. . . .

While I wondered again why I couldn't, wouldn't, didn't, with Fred Minckoff. (Catholic is as Catholic doesn't?)

Before leaving, Alice Bigboobs had them in Rolf's lap. He made no move to dislodge her. (Ah hah! Rolf has a girl?) That's why he's always screwed out by the time I get him? I mean, look around. They seem to love listening to *who he is*.

Rolf to me: You don't have any idea who I am.

Me to Rolf: There's not enough Geritol in the world to equip me for that kind of operation, you tyrant, I know who you are. . . . You're a party pooper, as we make our good-byes, off in the middle of Lolly's friend Tony's anecdote about how he and Fred Friendly almost had a good thing going. . . . You think I don't know who you are? You are a man who wants everything his way and gets it. You draw women like flies, and me along with them. You are an island unto yourself, only why don't you throw down a drawbridge every once in a while? You are also a terrible stuffed shirt, must you always lecture me, as we turn down Peck's Road long before the shank of the evening.

Rolf: "I'm telling you, you'll wake up one morning and find out you've frittered away your talents on nothing. End up like that little TV Lothario Lolly's found for you."

Which makes me laugh; all these years good as the golden rule and then sit for ten minutes talking to some wop as much like my Uncle Louis from Sicily to be my Cousin Louie from Elmhurst and he's jealous.

"We were talking about CBS. I can't even remember his name. He's got them interested in four ideas," I say to justify myself.

"Ideas?" he counters sarcastically. "Buy yourself a copy of *The Watchtower*, it's filled with ideas. The history of the Christian handkerchief. How to marinate a chicken turd, what do you mean, ideas? An idea is only as valid as the mind willing to do something with it . . . make it into something, you jerk, into something of value. Which is something CBS doesn't understand. So don't quote CBS to me, or any of your other New York pedigrees."

Rolf is now on another favorite subject (see Diary 1960, 1961, 1962, 1963, 1964, etc. for Rolf Edwards on subject of "New York pedigrees"). Pucci (pronounced, those pajama-looking dresses), Chateaubriand, Uptown, Cardin, Andy Warhol, Häagen-Dazs, thirty-dollar sunglasses and Bloomingdale's (New York pedigrees, all), this Artist of mine, with his mineral-deposit convictions. . . .

And I got horny.

Do me something, he drives me nuts but turns me on. This John L. Lewis of Form, Content, and Integrity, leaving a party because parties bore him, putting a halt to any discussion of "making it," maneuvering, the right places, people, or moves. Anything that even vaguely smacks of the way it's done. Why was I bothering to rub up against him? It was going to take more than my old meat loaf to get him to climb down off that soapbox.

"I'm trying to tell you something," he says, after I whispered in his ear, "Let's fuck." "When are you going to get your mind out of the seventh grade?" And I whispered back, "I'm trying to tell you something, too . . ." the sound of the yellow light up ahead searing my eyeballs.

He said, "The artist has to believe in himself." I said, "How about believing in us for a change?"

I can feel the back of his hand hit me hard between my seventh grade mentality and my thing. I've done it again. I've interrupted, lost his scent, and not paid attention to who he is.

"We're in trouble, Rolf," I almost say, but just then he touches me. Not sexy. No special meaning. Just the brush of his jacket when centrifugal meets centripetal around a curve, and I just want another one. Once more with meaning.

And I still want it an hour later when I get the dry humps and have to rub my breasts against the sheets. My husband has another woman in another pumpkin shell. How come it's as plain as the nose on his face and I don't blow it?

KATHERINE
A quarter of eight in the morning

I am asleep, I am not asleep. Rolf's hands suddenly have grabbed everything I always wanted them to, and I come four times by five after. Big and noisy, I can't understand why he doesn't reach out more often. Especially as I feel his volcanic release throb so hard I leave two red welts on his back where I've dug in my heels. Two golden tears on his eyes where I've glued myself to his eruption.

Practice does too make perfect, and when I get up I'm not sure about anything anymore. My husband does not have another woman. Whatever gave me that idea?

ANTONY
January 8, 1974

Modern Romances. Women walk to and fro, speaking of the Big O. Fifteen years ago my comrades and I fantasized the Perfect Woman: all she wanted to do was fuck. Beware of what you desire in adolescence, for you will surely get it in middle age. We comrades are paying for our fantasies now. Fucking Frankensteins waiting behind every bedpost. "Don't fall in love with me, just fuck me"—an actual quote from Linda before our first coupling. It is all supposed to come under the heading of the Turnabout of the Sexes.

Work is slow and money dwindling. Submitting story ideas to "CBS Playhouse" like mad. According to Terry, they think I am hot stuff down there. When was the last time I swore never to write another word for TV? The medium is the masochist.

Four more months to my thirty-fifth, easily the midpoint of my life. I think I took a wrong turn somewhere. I am running out of air.

KATHERINE
January 10, 1974

My life is surrounded by women; aunt, friends, and daughter. (Steig cartoon: "My mother loved me, but she died." Not funny. I miss her.) January 10, 1914, Mother was born. July 10, 1968, Mother loved me, but she died. I'm glad Christa knew her. I'm glad she knows the difference between Mother's lasagna and Chef Boy•ar•dee.

Christa said this morning, "I'm a much closer rela-

tive to Daddy than you are; how come I can't sleep
with him?" and don't throw Freud at me and then
Gesell. It's sad. Cause she wants to so much. I'm blue.
I'm going to St. Catherine's to light a candle. I'll call
Concetta; her life is surrounded by women, too. Sisters.
Some dead. And pretty soon it'll be my turn.

KATHERINE
January 11

Angela finally made it with the delivery boy. Or at
least he made it . . . all over her velvet pants. She was
hysterical. She can't wait for Sam to come back from
Cleveland. (To punish her?) (Oh, God, we're all
hanging off the deep end.)

KATHERINE
January 12

Christina Marie Edwards is growing up. My Christa,
for whom all this will be part of the olden days.
My Christa has her period!
"And whose little girl are you?" the nice man asked
her when she was a tiny, tiny child.
"I'm *my* little girl," she answered, knowing even
then what Angie, Dork, and I can't learn.
"What are you getting so excited about?" she wants
to know. "I'm practically the last one in my class and
next time get the Stayfree, Mom; Kelly says they're dy-
namite. . . ."
Who is this Kelly to put her two cents into my territory? Is it finished? My little girl and me? From now
on, once a month, sort of every twenty-eight days,
she'll write, in her own hand, in her own book: January 10, February 9, March 17. . . . Because she'll be

irregular at first. "You'll be irregular at first," I told her. "No kidding?" she answers, twelve years old, not even shrugging. "Next year you'll drop your first egg; it's nothing to worry about. Now you're one of the girls." She looks at me. Why didn't I keep my big mouth shut? Again, Kelly's beaten me to it.

"Don't be so gross," is all she can say as I stand there trying to ease her through one of life's big moments. "Just don't forget the Stayfree."

"And hang loose," she tells me, only it's lonesome, hanging loose all alone out there, but then, that's my problem, too, she tells me, and I suppose time will have its way with that score too. . . . after a time.

ANTONY
January 12

Spoke with Katey Edwards (spider lady from Prestons'). She has an interesting proposition. Seems she's got some publishers interested in a big novel about three generations of Rockefellers, oil, power, politics, and a cast of thousands. For reasons not altogether clear to me, she wants me to collaborate with her. There is probably an advance in it, including a partial, if I commit. I told her about my CBS project, but she says I can do both, do me good. She's an aggressive character. Fact is, a little collaborative work might do me some good at this point. And I've always promised myself a try at a big-book best-seller. Another lottery ticket.

Meeting Katey tomorrow night to discuss the project.

Lolly Preston's friend Tony (the writer—he's considering the book—I hope, I hope. Likes idea. Anyway, he's considering it). He came to dinner. Rolf in New York.

Tony Amato. Boy, does he remind me of home!

The F train from Rego Park.

Bet his old man collects Victor Red Seals: Caruso, Galli-Curci, Zinka Milanov. . . . El Verdo all right.

Manicotti on Sundays . . . a little saltimbocca . . . another helping of gnocchi? It's good for you, puts the roses in those cheeks.

Mass at eleven.

Tuesday night Rosary Society.

No surprises here. Tony could be brother Mike. We look so much alike I can feel his palms sweat.

I look at his dark face and wonder if that's the way he sees me. We're not American, he and I; we have a spy look. This Tony is overcast with stiff Korean hair and bushy eyes. I know I look like him. I am his double and we make me nervous.

Rolf's gone, but he's still here. He sits at my left hand. He sits at my right. I can graze other men's arms, pass them the salt, pour them wine, but I am forever separate. I am bespoke. . . . And I like it. (Tony said I have a life partner. He's right. He is, I think, a bit wistful. He's divorced. I run downstairs to write down "life partner." I'm afraid I'll forget it.)

Tony stayed late. One, one-thirty. We "got to know each other." Schools, neighborhoods. . . . Turns out he's not even from New York. His father owns a Sunoco station in Rye and wouldn't know *La Forza del*

Destino from Joey Gallo. And sure, but he's what
Newsweek calls your typical "swinger"; no, not typical,
he hates "hangouts," all those "Monday, Tuesday"
places. Mostly he makes it with his old married friends'
baby-sitters. (He was married six years. She was Italian, too, though talk about your typicals . . . like the
rest of us dark, brooding types, he also goes for the
long-legged Dutch. Germans. An occasional Irish col-
leen.) From the list of exploits he trotted out for my
approval, he seems to do all right—the long-legged Ol-
gas seem to go for their opposites, too. And I do mean
approval. I got the idea he felt he had to entertain me.
Or, if not entertain, then what? Show off? Let me see
what I'm missing?

ANTONY
January 13

Katey Edwards is a can of worms.
Folksy-frenzy dinner with her and her daughter.
Food was prepared short-order style, meat, rice, and a
vegetable stew that looked like the food-of-the-week-
in-review. All cooked behind the back while Kate carries on simultaneous conversations with me, her kid,
and various folks on the phone, including her hubby,
who is in New York. But these conversations seem interchangeable: She's finishing her conversations with
her husband with me, and discussing her tax situation
with her twelve-year-old daughter. The food looks
ugly. She looks crazy. I pity her husband. I keep thinking I can't possibly work with her—too many loose
ends.
Next—all business. She starts by saying my role will
be organization and plotting which she considers her
weaknesses. She says my background in TV should be
valuable, which I take as a dubious insult. Then, non-

stop, she proceeds to lay out the organization and plotting computer style, reducing me to a stenographer.
What she has in mind is a sort of *War and Peace*, pit-
ting Western oil family (Rockefellers) against Eastern
oil family (Shah of Iran), all spanning three generations, a hundred years, and sex on five continents. She
seems to have a master outline all in her head. She
has twenty-two characters in mind for starters. I am
dizzy. I have trouble juggling three characters in a
small room. During "all business," Katey is all mind
and mouth. I am impressed. Bonnie was wrong: Italians are smart Italians.

That finished, Katey brews a pot of coffee and asks
me about my sex life. No segue, just, "What's your sex
life like?"

I tell her it is like a fountain.

She tells me she is doing research.

I wonder if she is trying to seduce me, using the
same technique I failed with years ago. ("I think sex is
something one should be able to discuss openly and
without embarrassment, don't you, Matilda?" The first
in my series of turnoff openers.) But no, if Katey is after anything from me, it is fantasy material; she is picking my brain for masturbation plots and she also wants
me to assure her that the single life is lonely.

I tell her it is lonely, but that I still have a thing
about new bodies. I can see her filing that away for
some midmorning onanism.

Then I tell her about my predilection for Nordic
types, especially Nazis, to demonstrate just how lonely
I like it, and Katey gets visibly nervous. (It's hard to
tell when this lady is getting nervous, actually, because
it is all a matter of degree—she has an excessive energy problem.) The reason for her nervousness becomes apparent immediately: being a dark "mole" type
(as she puts it) like me, she has a thing for cool-
skinned beer drinkers herself. Note the All-American
surname on her hubby. She admits to worrying about

her tits (which are indiscernible under her oil-crisis sweaters) and her odd patches of body hair. She wants to know if Nordic ladies really do have silky pubic hair. I assure her that they do and she seems to sulk. Then I tell her that I've come across a few of those robust goddesses who couldn't come with a hydraulic hammer, and she is all smiles again. She seems to want to assure me that that isn't one of her worries. I can believe her. With that much nervous energy she can probably come sitting cross-legged on a subway.

The fact is, I like this woman. She seems, in this wilderness of my latest exile, to be a kindred spirit of sorts. All I meet up here are garden-variety neurotics, exurbanites who chat about their green thumbs and rejoice in their escape from New York as if they had come through a pogrom. Underneath, they're all planning triumphant returns to Manhattan. Katey probably dispensed with nonsense once and for all in the crib. She's pure wop, like me. I think we'll work well together, a real brother-and-sister act. And being mirror images, we can dispense with sex as another bit of nonsense.

KATHERINE
January 13—later

Christa very quiet during dinner, watching, like she used to from the carriage. Laser beams for eyeballs. That look in those lasers of hers. "I know more than you'll ever imagine, Big Mama, so get outa my way." Or is it still maybe, I hope, "I don't ever, ever in my whole life want to live anywhere but here; who is this man in Daddy's chair?"

My baby. My fat, little chunk, crawling through my lousy housekeeping. Now almost somebody else, sitting there watching a man through the bush of her father's yellow eyelashes. And that way she's learned of slapping them up and down against her flushed cheeks. (A TV tart, she's learnt by heart . . .)

My daughter, the flirt. But where did she learn it? Who showed her? One minute standing on her hands, her Angie Dickinsons up against the icebox, the next looking at Tony that way, that slinking smile half-hidden behind the look.

I'm scared. For whom? Her hard times and narrow escapes? Or is it that my time is running out on me? Two women in one house? And then there she is pushing all the salad to the other side of the plate and wants more pasta. Nothing can touch. Not the meat, not the greens, not the linguini, and she's still my baby after all, ready only for her chapter of *Great Expectations,* her night brace, and her mama's kiss.

ANTONY
January 20

For old times' sake, Franco, Anna, and my little namesake (called Tonito in my presence to give me some stature) came up for a one-night visit. Goethe clearly had German wives in mind when he made his pronouncement. It would take a divining rod to detect significance in my sister-in-law. That woman has built an entire philosophy on the size of her tits. It is a political philosophy: Power equals cup size.

"Franco, please, lower your voice. We're right here."

"But we're in the country, Anna. No neighbors."

With that, Anna lifts those D milk bags of hers off the kitchen table where she has been giving them a little nap and points them in Franco's direction. Suddenly, they are bazookas and Franco is silent.

(Or am I missing something significant here? Are Franco and Anna in touch with something primal that a smartass TV writer couldn't begin to comprehend? Maybe those aren't bazookas at all, but The Life Source itself she carries around on her chest. And when Anna zeros them in on Franco's consciousness, she is reminding him of the well-spring of all Wisdom. "Behold, Franco, I speak from the tit. Listen and be humble.")

On the other hand, Anna may simply be a pain in the ass. She sees a threat to her happy homelife in every move I make. If the phone rings, she turns up the radio so Franco won't be contaminated by the obscenities I must surely be pouring into the wire. And Franco, of course, is all ears.

Franco, leering: Who was that? A friend?

Me: A business associate. (Kate with some research leads.)

Franco gets off several winks.

Me: It was, Frank. I'm all business these days.

And more winks until Anna gives him a full view of the Life Source.

They left me, God bless them, with two thoughts on my mind:

One, I remember why I never remarried: there is too much significance in it for me at this late date.

And two, I remember why I am usually in the company of sunlit types these past few years. Oh, yes, they don't have half the significance of an Anna (or Bonnie, for that matter), but what they lack in intensity they more than make up for with mindless good cheer. After one day with Anna, my lungs ache for the airiness of Annamarie or Lena. Okay, so Annamarie is fully capable of eating an apple while I gnaw on her labials, but maybe that is healthiness! And I think it's infectious. Sitting under Annamarie's skirt, I find myself drifting into a Monet landscape. The thought of dealing with Anna's privates gives me the DTs; I see slabs of Francis Bacon meat and gnarled Soutine olive groves.

And yet I couldn't imagine actually living with Annamarie. Two days in a row and I'd be nothing more than a lily pad.

KATHERINE
January 17

4:00 A.M.—couldn't sleep. Spent a long time in front of mirror examining my body. Have I become no more than an uplift and a pair of satin mules? Has this obsession of mine become carnivorous and already swallowed the rest of me?

I'm sweating. All the windows are open, and stark naked, I'm dripping with the willies. Where is the us of yesterday, Rolf? I never used to haunt gas stations in the middle of the night, looking for enough regular to take me to Casablanca. Why are we sleeping back to back these years? Me lying in a pool of penultimate moments? Where has the old us gone to?

ANTONY
January 18

Good news: CBS loved my treatment.
Bad news: CBS canceling the show.
Tear up another lottery ticket.
Good news: The Rockefeller book is going swimmingly. Katey and I worked three hours tonight making a master plot chart that looks like a biology diagram. Then we spent another hour with our researcher, a flea-brained coed on vacation from Tufts, who makes me remember why I never got on with girls when I was a teenager. I'm sure Katey was more interested in her ice-cream-scooped tits than I was.

Then another half hour going over my library notes
with Kate-the-computer. She shuffles my facts and then
spews them out on three-by-five cards, all with coded
chapter numbers. For someone who gives every impression of suffering daily from petit mal, she certainly
can do her stuff. Ho-hee, maybe we'll get rich after all.

On the way out, I have a cup of coffee with the Mis-
ter. Rolf is a pleasant fellow, I'm sure, but every time I
run into him, I come away feeling like an underachiever, even though from the looks of things, old
Mr. Kate is having his problems bringing home the
bacon. He told me very confidentially that he's up for
some kind of a supergraphic mural in hard-edge New
York. (Why is it always these gentle, sensitive types
who go in for impersonal art? I think of Seurat burning
himself up with antipassion in his mommie's attic.) I
guess that's it: Kate's hubby is such a purist, I always
feel like a mudpie after these encounters.

Something endearing, though (or is it?). He says,
"*We* have been hoping for this mural." The familial
"we." Oh, how I envy him that (not Kate and Christa,
just the "we"). God help me, I'm a sentimentalist at
heart.

I'll bet they have a marvelous time in bed, if he can
get her to stop twitching while he gets it in. It's those
purist types who fuck like wild pigs. Maybe I'll ask
Kate— God knows, she's dug out enough about my
bedlife.

Part II

Big women's meeting at Carmelita's. They're still there. I drove over with Lolly Preston and borrowed her jeep to get out of there. Couldn't stand it. Hated it. Ran away, hiding, don't take me back.

Just read in Dear Abby: "Dear Abby, My husband never gives me any peace. I have to hide in the closet to change into my pajamas. If I just take off my socks in front of him he starts in with me. What should I do? Exhausted."

Dear Exhausted, you lucky bitch, just tell me what size socks you wear and how can I order a couple dozen?

Women's meeting depressed me so. I took notes. I spied. I was separate, depressed, and supercilious/envious.

A fat lady named Irene said, "Tee-hee, I'm the mad housewife."

A checked-flannel lady named Joan: "I just love lectures. My husband always fell asleep."

Maryanne from Freestone: "I just love people."

Nina Spence: "I dunno, do a little glasswork when the mood hits me."

Leader wearing Leader clothes, in Leader eyeglasses, said with authority: "Did you have something out of turn you'd like to ask? Would you all be comfortable with that?"

She was a "facilitator." Facilitators apparently memorize "Would you be comfortable with that?" All four facilitators said it a lot. Another one said, "Ask questions about me. You will learn to know yourself through knowing me." She smiled.

The unfacilitators, us ordinary oppressed women, said:

"I'm into nature."

"I'm good with my hands."

"I just want to help people."

Some nameless somebody said, "You're afraid of losing by grasping too much."

I got sick. I got into Lolly Preston's jeep and came home to look for Rolf. A man, any man. *Now that's what I'd be comfortable with!* Just to stand next to and be different from. Run my tongue over his body to prove I, too, could "do something for others." I wanted back whatever I gave—back and back some more. Lick and be licked.

As I drove, my breath got tight. I counted backward from the eighth. If I was on time that's when it ought to come, when I was scheduled to fall off the roof (not supposed to say, "fall off the roof"). When I'd get the curse. (Not supposed to say that, either.) Supposed to be glad all over it's validity-of-sex time again. Anyway I counted backward. Did I dare go on to the studio without stopping home for the diaphragm? It was ten days to the eight. Exactly, no leeway, which made it iffy, awfully iffy. What if I got caught? Thought of Christa, teeny tiny with Mazola all over her baby's ass. Thought of the great American novel nobody would ever bother to read even if anybody ever wrote it. Thought of Rolf and decided to keep on driving.

Turned down Mole Road too fast. If he knew how much I wanted him, he'd be ready when I got there, facing the door with a showstopper between his legs.

Our jeep was in the driveway and I left Lolly's on the hard-top, climbed the 134 steps to the glass studio we built instead of insulating the bedroom.

"Honey?" Me, running toward him. Him looking up startled over cadmium blue.

"What's the matter?" he asks me, thinking of disaster first. Chris, then the rest of us down to his rich uncle back in Elgin.

"Nothing," I said, throwing myself on him. "Just hold me, everything's terrific."

"I'm holding you. Kathy, what's the matter?"

"You'll be mad."

"I won't be mad, Kathy; why should I be mad? I thought you went to the women's—"

"I left."

"Kathy?"

"Let's . . . Rolf, let's just go lie down."

Suspicious flesh hardening like refrigerated fat on the top of spaghetti sauce.

"No." I winced, but he said it anyway. "For crissakes, Kathy, you're flipping out with this nympho routine of yours," and I knew I was whimpering.

"What do you think I do here all day? Sit in the john jerking off? Christ, Kathy, if you're that hard up get yourself a job in the Last Chance Saloon as a B-girl, but leave me the hell out of it so I can get some work done."

Out of it? Listening to the gnashing of my back teeth.

He asks me if I think he's a soap machine. "Two dimes for a pack of problem softener?" and then his plea for someone who's just generally affectionate and doesn't expect him to Last Tango her to ecstasy at the wiggle of a tit.

"I mean it," he hollered, holding me out from him as if I had scarlet fever. "Don't expect me to be a trained seal with an instant hard-on every time you think you're Theda Bara." And there it was, finished, not only my Saturday afternoon revel but the illusions. That somehow I hadn't ever heard the message before. Rolf has no intention of renewing his subscription to

Art in America. He's given up on it, along with his eagle scout badge, bent-pin fishhook, and collection of Marvel comics.

"It won't happen again, I promise," I promised. "I'm sorry," and I was. And I was crying and I wanted to drown and jump in front of a car and auction myself off to the Salvation Army.

Was I really? The kind that ends up on the barroom floor?

"Hey," he was calling after me, "maybe we can . . ." except I didn't listen. What? Recycle us like yesterday's Tab?

Hell, Rolf, you contracted. Now either pay attention or get off my pot. Him shouting for me to come back, as I started in third and went into overdrive before I was even out onto the road.

And this time it wasn't just, "I want a lover," I screamed as I drove along. This time I said to myself maybe what I really want is a divorce.

ANTONY
January 19

Did I say Kate Edwards was a can of worms?

How about a can of snakes?

When am I going to learn to trust my snap judgments?

And have I mentioned lately that I am the easiest lay in Upstate New York?

To begin at the beginning: Katey came over today to work on the plot chart. Gave me an hour's notice which was fine with me. I'd done my homework and was looking forward to it. Had a big pot of coffee going when she scrambled in. I choose the word "scrambled" advisedly. She was in true spider-lady form. Or maybe a jackrabbit. She had just been to church, she said. I told her she was a good girl. She screamed she wasn't. I handed her a cup of coffee, much of which still remains on my once-yellow sofa.

I said, "You seem a bit jumpy. . . . Maybe you should return to religion gradually instead of leaping in like that."

She said, "Fuck you."

I said, "Let's get to work."

I think she said "Fuck you" again, but I'm not sure, because she was soon crying. Not little weepy stuff like I'm used to from my Nordic sentimentalists, but sobs. Oh, God, she cried the way I dream of crying. And I think I started to, too, sympathetic little sniffles. I have never been much good as a witness to full-out emotion; my line has always been the halfhearted stuff.

"Jesus, Katey, what's this? Please, God, tell me."

But she just took my hand and squeezed it until it throbbed. I guess I held her then. I didn't know what to do. I like Katey. I'm really not used to seeing that much naked pain. That much rawness.

Was it the rawness that turned me on? (Yes, we fucked—but that's not the half of it.) Rawness? That usually turns me off. Or the vulnerability? Was it one of my famous Zorba-never-turns-an-aching-woman-down fucks? Jesus God, I don't know. My head is still boggling. There was something too close, too sudden about it. I'm used to planning my fucks. At least having a fantasy or two in private before I get to it. And honest to God, I never once fantasized fucking Katey. Never crossed my mind. And I liked it that way. Thought it would be bad for business (which, strangely, I don't think it will be now). But apart from that, I never thought of fucking Katey because I really don't like the way she looks. And there's a simple reason for that: she looks like me. And I don't like the way I look.

I don't know when the crying and comforting stopped and the grabbing and scratching and tearing and pounding started and which came before we went upstairs and which after. And if I said anything, it was from a script from some other, rehearsed fuck, not this wildcat thrashing. And if she said anything, I couldn't hear it.

Katey Edwards does not have any orgasm problems.

I think she may have some marital problems, but I didn't ask.

We fucked in fast motion. A jittery spasm fuck the likes of which I've never known. At one point, I was afraid of losing consciousness.

And then we fucked in slow motion. And the spider-lady-mole-jackrabbit-contortionist made love impersonating a faun. I give her full credit. She is a transformation artist.

She is a goddamned lovemaking artist.

And I feel goddamned peculiar just now.

After the slow motion, after the cigarette, after several smiles and looks that came from the same place as the tears, Katey Edwards suggested that we still had time for a little work. And, by God, we dressed and came downstairs and filled out coffee mugs and charted out Rocky's years at Dartmouth and then she went home, giving me a winking kiss at the door and saying something typically Katey in four unfinished sentences about how she felt better than when she came in and discretion is the better part of dinner at her house next week and would I read up on oil rigs good-bye.

I'm sure this is an unrepeatable afternoon and that's okay with me.

I'm sure that life is an unfathomable adventure that I wouldn't trade in for any imaginable alternative.

And I'm sure that Katey Edwards has more going on in that little dago body and mind of hers than could be dreamed of in my philosophy. I hope she is okay.

Oh, God, I've come from Tony's. Church or no church, nothing will ever change that.

Breasts hurt all the way there. I wasn't wearing a bra and the nipples were raw from rubbing against the fisherman's weave. Half the buttons were undone and it was all so calculated. I kept watching him. Did he know the minute I came in? I was hoping I didn't know, but I did. Oh, God, I knew all right.

I finally got him to sit down, with the coffee with the something to munch, all so okay-now-to-workish, but the room swam in sun yellows and sculptured green rug and piles of newspaper for the fireplace and wood and Tony and me suddenly crying, like I do all the time now, everything swimming in a white paper Azuma shade, him looking like me, me like him. "Come on," he tells me, only I don't listen. My skirt's getting wet. I'm crying over the both of us, in this bachelor, fuck-everybody room where I have no business being.

"It's okay," he keeps saying. "Let it out. I've been there." And I can feel myself clinging to him. He feels hard and I weld myself in closer. We reflect each other in our eyes, he and I; he is Mike; he is me: we are Sicily.

"I can't help it," I'm moaning, hanging on to him. "Tell me it's not my—" but before I can even think "fault," his tongue has pushed mine out of the way. I'm choking on it. His hands are being my brassiere. He's cradled my head into his so that we are Siamese. The room is sweating, burning. I can't tell if it's me or everything that's so spastic and frantic. I am desperate, to fall down his throat, to be soldered to his skin. I know that I have wound myself around him with pincers. His mother couldn't have distinguished flesh from flesh.

"Let's" he said. "Mmmmmmmmmsure." Sure, let's, I don't care what it is, if it's doable, do me; only all he wants to do is go upstairs. He's already standing. I hang on him, I cling, *Don't* leave me. Tony. Finish. Finish. I am chugging like my Saab with its out-of-gap points. Up the stairs, through rooms, squeezed together, foot on toe, instep on earlobe.

"You don't understand," I kept muttering, grabbing for him, never getting enough. "You don't understand, I am a respectable woman; I am here under false colors, in with bad company . . ."

His iron bar bursts up through my palm, growing into my wristbone. My legs get weak and strong with one spasm. It was all lost, the getting upstairs. In a new room, out of clothes like Clark Kent, writhing like four gyroscopes. His finger in my mouth, my tongue like a small snake eating, wet and dry, sloppy. Very sloppy, coming again, again, coming puttputtputt, the little engine that could forever, don't stop me, again, again, higher and meaner. I come against two fingers, around his tongue, hard like a Good Humor. Quiet in his arms. Heavy, dangling, jiggle me on top of you. With him, two together, one big noise, screaming till my bladder pains, while he lies there, rolls over and plays dead, eyes staring up all whites into the ceiling.

And then there's a still quiet that is shattered by the sound of a female scream. It must be me. Me screaming because down there my animal will not stop. It is pushing between exhaustion and hunger. The sound has become supersonic. It's deafening to both of us. And still the gnawing, yowling deeper and deeper convulsions jab icicles up under the fingernails of my heart.

KATHERINE
January 20

I am shit, not good enough to look into the eyes of
my child or anywhere near her. I can't believe what
I've done.

KATHERINE
January 21

Lovely snow out today. Inside, warm as a mongrel,
read Dickens from breakfast to nightfall. The joys of
early retirement.

KATHERINE
January 25

I polish Rolf's boots, take in the shirts, clean out his
drawers, listened and listened last night to everything
he said, thinking, Dirty seconds, dirty seconds, you
sneak, you bitch, you sneaky deceiving bitch, how
could you?

"Spam steak again? Twice in one year? How come?"
Because my lover is coming to dinner. Because it's
your favorite and inedible, cornball, milltown, low-
class, boring, and will make me look dumb and unso-
phisticated, and low in his eyes and he doesn't know

it's your favorite, and dear God, don't let Rolf find out, and dear God, because I did it one time that doesn't make him my lover, please, please forgive me, if I live through this meal I will walk on my knees to Hackensack, New Jersey, and had I known that last week I would disgrace my life, my man, my lawfully wedded love, would I have ever, in my wildest dreams said, today to my partner (that's all he is, my writing partner), would I have said to him, come here for dinner first? First? Before writing. Working. The book. Oh, my God, how can I do this with him anymore? Face him? Across the table? And Rolf's second favorite—candied yams . . . Eat them, Jezebel, gain forty pounds. Suffer. You, oh, dear God, protect me. What's wrong with me? Why the hell am I doing this?

ANTONY
January 25

I am thinking tonight of the passage of time, of its irreversibility, and of the blooming fact that in a few months I will be thirty-five.

Such thoughts follow directly, I guess, from tonight's session with Kate. She invited me over for dinner before our work. And who should be the guest of honor but her hubby. No doubt, this was Katey's way of letting me know that Saturday's little adventure was strictly out of context. And by God, how I envy her context. Rolf is a man of grace and purity, an artist with an artist's heart, and if he does not always screw his little missus on schedule (which I now think must have been the origin of Katey's case of vaginal nerves the other day), then it is because he is a romantic who probably loves her more than her horny little heart deserves. Kate played up her wifeyness, serving Rolf first, guiding dinner conversation like a good shepherd, almost picking his teeth for him. And for some reason he was trying hard, too, trying to tell me with laughs and smiles that he has no objection to my being a writer with a whore's mentality although, of course, that isn't his line. In another frame of mind, I could have resented him—and sure, I can imagine it gives Kate the willies when she'd like to play the whore rather than the angel—but tonight I liked Rolf fine. And if I feel judged by him, it is because time has passed and I don't have a wife or child or even the pure heart that denying same should provide for me.

Kate and I put in a couple of good hours on the book and seem to be ready to try a couple of sample chapters. There were, of course, no references to Saturday.

I didn't feel guilty in front of Rolf. It's funny, on the occasions when I have been the "other man," I never viewed the husband as the cuckold. Usually I feel some sort of kinship to him which, no doubt, is written off as homosexuality in the textbooks. On the other hand, when I've been cuckolded, I feel like one through and through. Ho hum.

KATHERINE
January 26—night

Didn't get up with Chris this morning. Three dreams to try and catch before they got away. Too late. But spent a long time thinking about Rolf. About Guilt. About the whys. Last night. The other night. And how come he had his hand on my ass when Tony was there and turned over to go to sleep when Tony wasn't there?

ANTONY
January 29

A hot cunt has no conscience.

Or is there something else going on here?

Tonight I am covered with semen and cunt juice and shame. And I am filled with longing for some *innocent* romance.

Katey again.

We worked like ants on our sprawling project from eight to twelve at her place. Details. She's a regular tax accountant when it comes to filling in the minutiae of the novel, from the style of the mantel on John D.'s salon fireplace to the shape of an oil drill bit. She knows where to fit it all, a pleasant surprise for both of us. So we worked. And we worked together well, as always. Never dropping a stitch. Two little computers working in dialectic. Collaboration has never been so productive for me, so hassle-free.

This was my thought as I left her place and got into my car—what fine collaborators we are. And then, as I turned on the ignition, I see her jackrabbiting out the door with some papers in her hand. She rushed around to the other door, climbed in, and said I had forgotten my carbon of something or other. (I hadn't.)

Thanks, I said. And then I made some comment about how well we work together.

Katey said, "Yes, that's true. And I think I'd like to suck your cock now."

Just like that. No segue. She hops from A to Z as if B through Y were too obvious to mention.

And so do I. My cock was out and bobbing happily next to the gearshift in one second, and her hot wop mouth was around it in the next. The car was running. Christa was snoozing twenty feet away from us in the

54

house. Rolf was due to roll up the driveway at any minute. And there was Katey gobbling away at my prick like a starving Armenian, the gearshift vibrating between her little breasts, the carbons still in one of her hands. And she is groaning so hard I can feel it reverberating in my balls as she comes over and over again while I sit there stupefied, my hands still on the steering wheel, staring stupidly straight ahead.

And then we are in the back seat, bouncing around like frantic teenagers, our clothes half off, gasping, scratching, pouncing, until I come so hard I am sure I am dying. It's all over. My heart has stopped in the back seat and I can imagine Katey clambering out, releasing the brake, and rushing back into the house to start cooking a stew so she can be stirring domestically when the police arrive.

I do not die. I pull myself together and somersault back into the driver's seat. I leave Katey grinning in her driveway, carbons still in hand.

And I drive home feeling like a sullied little girl. A very excited sullied little girl. .

I moved to the country for solace.

KATHERINE
January 30

I have reached bottom. (I love it.) I do. I am sick. Bottom is muddy and slurpy. You get to wallow in it and squoosh it between your privates—Yich.

We worked, Tony and I, at our place, Rolf out. We worked like two little A students. We are writing a book. We are . . . liar . . . after working I went out and screwed the bastard right in the middle of my own driveway. I am without shame, morals, or common sense.

New York has lost its charm. I'm down to do some research for the book and usually such an expedition would be titillating. Fact is, I longed for home the minute I got here.

Even the subway ride was without a thrill. There was a time when I saw more stories between stops than in a volume of Chekhov: A Puerto Rican secretary about to embark on a dangerous love affair with a black ambulance driver; an old Czech hallucinating that the train has been stalled by bandits; a Hasidic messenger boy catching himself in a dream about his sister. Nothing doing today. Today, my fellow passengers all appear to have been bitten by an underground tsetse fly. From the looks of things, we all could be on a cargo train for Dachau. I tried an old game: at gunpoint I am required to pick a wife from my car before Fourth Street. But I can't do it. Not even the miniskirted Chinese student will do, she with her Columbia notebook tight against her stomach. Nope, the fantasy will not sustain; in a month, she is telling me that I am insensitive to the Romantic poets and I am yelling back that she has forsaken her culture which knew more than to produce a Byron. By Fourth Street, we have gotten a quiet annulment and I am alone again, facing the Jefferson Market Library, a free man.

At night, I have scallops and broccoli at Gene's and Marsha's. Gene's scallops, Marsha's broccoli. Everything is split down the middle in this house, separate bank accounts, separate clothes hampers. There was a time when I admired these two for the neat way they made their marriage survive. Bonnie and I even tried to model ourselves after them that last desperate year.

(Hey, Tony, you did try, didn't you, old boy? Remember that next time you got the Everything-I-Touch-Turns-to-Shit Blues.) But somehow tonight I'm not in the mood for their neatness. They've got it down to a syntactical science: never does the word "we" escape their lips. Occasionally a contorted sentence like "Both Gene and I saw *Passions of Anna* the other night."

"Together?" I ask.

"In a sense," says Gene. "But it certainly was a different experience for each of us."

Oh, yes, I'm sure it was, friends.

Over Grand Marnier, we get down to basics. I am asked if I have read Masters' and Johnson's latest sci-sex potboiler.

"Just the dirty parts," I say.

I am told that there was a time when I was good for a serious discussion. I beg each of their pardons.

"Both Marsha and I have just completed our first set of encounters."

"How's that?"

It seems my old friends are the first on their block to be getting sex therapy from two of M. & J.'s New York missionaries.

"Well, uh, that sounds nice." There are intimacies and there are intimacies. I have no trouble asking a perfect stranger if she'd like to take a bath with me, but somehow I get squeamish when married folks so much as mention the conjugal bed. Must have something to do with Mommy and Daddy. (Last time we talked about it, Franco still insisted that the folks had only done it twice, once for each of us.)

But, lo, Gene and Marsha must tell all: how they spent a week just "pleasuring" each other, no insertion allowed; and then a week watching each other masturbate, just as a refresher course; and finally, the Big Time, complete with a stopwatch.

"It's like learning anything else." Gene tells me

proudly. "I had six years of Latin, but until now, no-body ever taught me how to fuck."

"Really fuck," adds Marsha, without so much as a grin.

"Golly," says I, "I bet I've been doing it wrong all these years."

And so, apparently, ended a nine-year friendship.

I wanna go home.

KATHERINE
February 2

"Someday you'll know," my mother said to me a long time ago after I'd spent the day complaining I wasn't blond. Complaining I wasn't lanky and lithe and lean and off a subway poster for filter cigarettes.

"I want to be American," I'd wanted. I wanted to be Rolf and Fred Minckoff and Annabel Lyng and Coke and french fries, both of which give me heartburn. I'd hardly even go out with an Italian.

Does sleeping with an Amato equal going out?

And my mama was right. Someday I did know. Someday wop *was* beautiful, me into the bargain! Korean hair, blue shadows under the eyes, brown haze around the fingernails, aureoles, elbows. Someday I did look out at the blond world and say the hell with you. Just because you don't eat garlic, don't think you're such hot stuff. The only hot you are is ice. And you stink on it.

We are hot.

Tony and me.

We are the hottest, horniest, h. . . . . . .

We are a hot item. Ticket.

We are despicable. Sour grapes. I ought to take sleeping pills.

Another day at the library going over Upton Sinclair and the *Petroleum Journal*. After four hours I am of the opinion that John D. deserves every penny he digs out of the earth. I have an unshakable admiration for any form of monomania. Also, I unearthed a strange irony: oilmen are naturalists at heart, which should come as a surprise to my local eco fiends. Yup, scratch an oilman and you find a man who likes to stick his hands in the soil, to burrow around in the earth like a weasel. Mineral farmers, they are. Groundbreakers.

Tonight I ate alone at Stanley's Cafeteria, one of my favorite pastimes (I haven't yet broken my rule of not taking anyone there with me). Not a word of English in the place: Yiddish, Salvic, an occasional German word, and just a touch of Spanish. I was the youngest there by twenty years. I'm sure this place has more intellectual vibes zinging than the smoker of the Harvard Club. (Come to think of it, the few times I've smoked in that smoker the only vibes I felt were money vibes.) I felt lovely over my goulash and rice.

Back at Leo's (he's in Hollywood) still high from Stanley's, my mind turns quickly to sex and I spend a while "pleasuring" myself with thoughts of Kate dancing like sugarplums in my head. Funny, but in a way I resented her, the way she intruded spread-eagled into my mind without so much as a how-do-you-do. Takes me for granted, she does, even when I'm out of town. I've always thought masturbation was a private affair (better not tell Gene and Marsha). From the very start, when Dick Mobillio (my Masters) taught me the fundamental one-two method of onanism, I resisted the school of thought which insisted you had to bring a pinup (yup, that's what we called them then) to the bathroom with you for the one-two. Rocco said that if you didn't you'd end up a pervert. He may be right. No matter how active I am (like since Kate started our work-and-play system), I still like a little solo jacking off once in a while. It gives me a sense of uniqueness. Just me and my pal whiling away an hour. How about some privacy, Kate?

KATHERINE
February 4

If I am coming apart Christa doesn't notice. I am a model mother. I rise smiling and mix soy, cornmeal, bulgur and Maltex for a healthy, nutritious start of another fun-filled, exciting learning experience for her. I pick her up at 3:20 for the trip to Dr. Millionaire, our local teeth-prettier. I gently but unobtrusively prod for details of her day at school. I want to be there when she needs me. I need the sound of her enthusiasm to rub into my psyche like Jergens.

"Seth's impossible, absolutely impossible," she says.

"Oh?"

"You should see him, he's horrible."

I have seen him. Her description is not far from my own. But then, I also remember Louis Modics, from kindergarten back on Woodside Avenue.

"What did Seth do today?" I ask, and then shift into fourth and listen all the way to town.

"Well . . . First he rubbed this orange into my face and then he wouldn't let me into the room. You know the way you hold the door with your feet? And Mrs. Rabinowitz was coming, and he knew I didn't have my history done because he'd made a 747 out of it and sailed it through the study hall and then he went like he was singing, you know, only it wasn't a real song? 'I love Chris, she's so wonderful,' all that stuff, you know? Only it wasn't even a real tune and all. And he's horrible, I almost died, and then Mrs. Rabinowitz didn't see us, but he turned on the switch and then I turned it off and then he turned if off and I turned it on. I can't remember which. Anyway, and then he turned it off and I turned it on and then Mrs. Rabinowitz went, "Okay, Seth, that'll be enough" and then he let her in, only he tripped me. And it was so funny. Oh, God, I almost died. God! It was *so* funny!"

"He's nice, Seth. Do you like him?"

"Seth Kesten? Do I *like* Seth Kesten?"

Don't ask her again. One more octave higher and the windshield will shatter.

"You don't like him."

"Oh, Mom! Don't be so gross."

All of which is the same exact replay I lived through myself not so long ago. It is written for me to say, "Do you like him?" And for her to call me "gross." And then I have to play dumber and she has to call me that, too. And when she says, "Oh, Mom, sometimes you're so DUMB," I'm so grateful for the *sometimes* I buy her a double dip, she picks the flavor and I don't even get a lick.

Bad women can be good for some things.

ANTONY
February 5

"Let's fuck first." Katey coming in my kitchen door.

"And get it out of the way?"

"Yup."

"Either way's okay with me."

"Then let's fuck first." Katey is grinning from ear to ear.

"Or we could even skip it for that matter."

"I'd rather not skip it, darling, if it's okay with you." And with that she leads me up to the bedroom where we engage in a cheerful screw, a casual coupling like old, familiar farm animals on a sunny day.

After which she says, "I think we do it together rather splendidly," slips into her togs, and again leads me, this time down the stairs, to work on "Boulder."

Work goes fine, effortless, and after a couple of hours of it, Katey says, "Let's knock off and go upstairs again."

Which we do, etc.

And then, for the first time, we actually talk about what is going on.

Katey tells me that our collaboration has turned out to be "nifty" (her word).

I tell her the pleasure is all mine.

She insists that it is hers as well.

I tell her that free-lance writing has it all over office work and she says the same goes for free-lance lovemaking. By this remark I assume she means she has always combined the two, but she says something by way of an ambiguous denial. Then we agree that we are both terribly mature and liberated and undeluded without, of course, being heartless. Then Katey goes home, blowing me a satirical kiss from her car window.

Well, Tony, old boy, what is going on here?

I honestly don't know. The answer is muddier than usual. Muddy without being perplexing. Confusing without being disturbing. For sure, this Katey thing is something new for me. It's real without being routine. And dramatic without being melodramatic. And this compartmentalizing of work and play does not seem artificial. It seems . . . "nifty."

I feel happy and free today. I admit it. Damned happy.

This Katey Edwards is good for me. Instructive.

Rain. In a lot, playing seeing-eye dog with my life. Sniffing out where I've been, and where I'm headed for with my bloomers on fire.

I love you, Christa, you are my flesh and life. We are each other. But where is my mama? And do I just yearn to "come home again, Mama"? Is that Tony Amato's appeal? Do I want to be able to BE YOU? To grow old into your flesh? To spatter my cheeks with tomato sauce all the time and be proud of it? Mama, talk to me. Tell me, who do I turn to now that your back is turned? Mama, I'm not finished needing you, and who else can answer me? I called Angela and Dorcas. I got wrong numbers and busy signals. My life is surrounded by women but there's only one mother per customer.

I wonder if women with living mothers have diaries.

I am glad I have a daughter. One day I will hold her breasts against mine and then I will be my mother and she will have answered me. I think I don't want to look at Rolf Edwards because of the blond freckles under his chin, on his back, down his legs. I only want to pour myself into the rickety legs of my stunted lover.

You are me, so I become my mother, Tony Amato.

What is this thing called LOVE?

And it isn't *anybody* feeling you up, or getting you down under him. It's connected to the sex, sure, but mightn't it also be that the sex's connected to the other?

Is, in fact.

Stimulation number two.

Do Rolf and I talk anymore? I mean about anything. The eighty-unit old-age home going up at the Four Corners? Cyprus? Do we even, for heaven's sake,

talk about ingrown toenails? About what'ya do today?
Wanna go to the pitcher show?

Have we passed ten words between us all week
besides turning up the Aquastat, the price of mor-
tadella, Chris's midyear hockey standing?

That kind of stimulation!

Tony talks to me.

We lie in bed afterward and he wants to know it all.
From way back to before First Communion.

How long was I when I was born? (High forceps.)
And, just because I told Rolf fifteen years ago, there's
still a kind of high in telling Tony all over. And how
he got locked in a trunk, and was rescued only because
he owed his brother two bits, who therefore had a mo-
tive for finding him.

I want to know about that kind of detail. Rolf's I
know by heart.

That is also stimulation.

For instance, Tony watches stars. Starboard from
port. Mass, line, tension Rolf sees Art, always Art.

A blue streak. Tony and I. This talking. New sub-
jects.

I think that's part of it. I think it isn't only the sex
I've been starving for. I think maybe after a while you
need to take a couple of left turns just so your signal
hand doesn't fall off.

At least that's what I think today.

ANTONY
February 8

I lost my virginity today.

We left John D. drilling in Tulsa and began sucking
on each other's fingers. And biting. And scratching
each other's palms. Scratching, biting, groaning. Then
arms. And legs. Biting, scratching, licking. Minutes.

Hours. Katey ripping at the hairs on my thighs with tiny bites, pulling at the hairs on my balls. Then swallowing them one at a time and all but clamping down, her fist grinding into my ass, then one, two fingers shoving, stretching, reeming inside me. And she's making sounds I've never heard, like voodoo words, speaking in tongues. Tongues. Tongues curling in each other's asses, flicking like vipers'. And always pulling, tearing at each other's skin. Not a word. Just this, on and on. On the floor, groveling. More. More. And then we are rip-sucking each other. Cannibalizing prick and cunt. We are raw. This is lower than instinct. We are not mating. We are not feasting. We are chewing each other to bits. There will be nothing left. And no need for anything left. We are erasing each other.

I had one last thought—after this, I will never again be able to distinguish between pleasure and pain.

And then I fainted. She sucked until I was empty and I could not see anymore. I was out as if I had been clubbed.

But, goddamn it! What is this, Kate? What in the name of Life is this? When I awoke—minutes later?—she was above me at the table, typing up notes. She winked. ·

Can the same woman both feel more and *less* than any other person I've known?

KATHERINE
February 9

TONY. Smart but essentially sparkless. I think Rolf's got him beat here. Or maybe Rolf's not so smart.

I think I better not start this debit/credit ledger. It's ugly.

Genuinely, painfully miserable. Rolf's side of the

bed personless. He's gone away somewhere even though he's still here. I have gone away somewhere? I miss him. I want him.

Rolf, *Why don't you want me anymore????????????* Is it possible a husband can have another woman and a wife deliberately doesn't notice?

KATHERINE
February 11

Miserable. Went to Rolf's glassy studio with hot cocoa. He wasn't there. Where does he go when he doesn't go where he goes?????? Why isn't my husband my same old regular husband I married?

HELP!

MIDDLE AGE: Comes in like a cat, out like a light, on cat's paws, COMES.

Later—

Chris made biscuits. I helped. She liked it and me. Can't tell anymore which makes sense, coming or going, Rolf or Tony, me or me. . . . A dispassionate observer might say I was ambivalent. All the instruments agree on the husband's other woman. What is wrong with the husband's wife?

Called Tony as soon as she left. Said we had to talk about April 1950 *Fortune* article. We didn't.

Rabbits have nothing on us. We fuck enough to supply Easter bunnies for every kid in Cleveland. (I hope you read this, Rolf Edwards. Read it and weep. For the TWO OF US!)

ANTONY
Lincoln's Birthday

Up early to answer the ringing phone. It's a lady
named Lillian, a local schoolmarm to demented children in the Albany school system. Lilly (whom I met
by accident) has an exotic surname (Pamonola),
claims to be a quarter Algonquin Indian, and has a
handsome chest. I can think of nothing else that recom-
mends her, especially not her heartfelt concern for "un-
derachieving" children. And yet, when she tells me it is
a school holiday and she thought she'd drive down, I
dutifully invite her to lunch which, of course, will include a roll in the sofa for dessert. I thought I was ugly
as a child: I have no other reason for my promiscuity.
But at thirty-five, it's a stinking excuse. I waste too
much time and energy trying to be more blond than
Olaf.

So I gave Lilly whats-what an order after our
sardine sandwiches when, for the second time that day,
the phone rings and a female says, "Hello." 'Twas
Katey with a paragraph to read me because she wanted
to know "if it was too good" for our book. I had to cut
the conversation short because I was entertaining. I am
nothing if not gallantly promiscuous. Katey sounded
amused. Good old Katey, I thought, and told her I'd
call her back.

After Lilly left, I worked through dinner and then
remembered to call Kate:

Me: Hi. Sorry I couldn't talk before. Let's hear that
paragraph now.

Kate: Shove it.

Me: I beg your pardon?

Kate: Shove it up your guinea ass, Tony boy. . . .

Me: What do you mean, "boy"?

67

Kate: I mean you lack the wisdom of a full-grown man.

Me: I'm an underachiever.

Kate: *Au contraire*. Methinks you are an overachiever. And an overcompensator.

Me: It's only because I'm lacking in natural talent.

Kate: Your natural talent is about the only thing you have going for you.

Me: If it's okay with you, I think I'll hang up now.

Kate: Fuck you.

KATHERINE
February 12

Mad. Fucking mad, that fiend . . . What am I, his confessor? Okay, so he screws around, I know he screws around, who cares what he does? I don't need to hear the hairy particulars . . . his sauerbraten sweeties . . . let him keep his Olympic records to himself . . . which is not to say I care. I do not care who this man screws. This man is a free agent. This man does not owe me a thing, the rat. Cringing, ungrateful rat. . . . The thing is, after the other night I don't see how he could . . . Rolf's never seen me like that; writhing around like a snake pit . . . arms, limbs, trunk, fingertips, whipping around like . . . like, well what's the difference, I was naked. Really naked, maybe for the first time, while that Bessie Smith, Bill Bailey no-good, two-timer worked me over with that plugged-in penis of his. I was no different than a trained seal. Whatever he wanted . . . and now Freidle Frumdummer or whatever her name is . . . He does THAT to me and then Freidle Schnizelburger? I don't even think I like him. I *don't* like him; he is basically cold and dispassionate, an Alain Resnais movie, You are, my Stromboli-Rossellini . . . I'm dying . . . I'll call Dr. B.

Rolf on Dr. B.: Dr. B. is a psychiatrist: therefore Dr. B. is an asshole.

Rolf on Roget on Psychiatrist: Psychiatrist: shrink, one who tells your tales after school. He who burns up his petty professional competitiveness on the tennis court at his patient's expense. He who sits there like an asshole, says nothing, and gets away with it. While you pay through your sinuses.

Didn't say much at dinner. Rolf doesn't notice that I don't say much. That I'm eating different entrails these days. He never does . . . notice anything I do or don't do, which makes for a natural camouflage for my missing person, except that I HATE IT. Which is why I now have to worry about my lover's lover. If you'd noticed in the first place, I wouldn't have a damn lover. . . .

No making love tonight. Tonight I don't love you. And as for screwing? Solve first our immediate communications breakdown and then we'll see. . . . And then we'll see the error in that way.

Rolf does have a secret. I am sure of it. I am afraid of it. Somehow I don't believe it's just a woman.

Something is bothering him. I can feel the hair on the sides of his legs tremble against mine until it's almost two and he finally falls asleep so it's okay for me to.

Except I can't.

I lie there and feel in my bony heart that he is keeping something either between us or from me. Something either awful or embarrassing. Something.

Two-thirty I get up, go out, and drive into town. I am aware as I drive that I'm about to commit an act of disloyalty somehow different from all the others. I am running away from involvement with my husband's life. Before, wasn't it just running toward my own? (An essential difference.)

I drive faster and loathe myself. I drive fast enough

to crash. Into the sleeping town where I parked and got out to use the phone. Decided I'd hang up after three rings, my palm so sweaty I dropped the phone before I had the chance.

"Hello, hello . . ." The sound of his voice as the receiver banged against the wall of the booth.

"Hi. It's me."

"Who? Kate, is that you? What's the matter?"

"Why does something have to be the matter? I just called, that's all. Nothing's the matter."

"At two o'clock in the morning, you just called?"

"Why? Who are you with now?"

"With? Katey, it's ten after two. What's wrong?"

"I told you. I just wanted to talk. How are you?"

"I'm asleep. That's how I am."

"With whom?"

"Oh, for godsake, with my hand down my pajama leg, who do you think, with whom?"

"How should I know?"

"Kate? Is Rolf listening to this?"

"I'm in town."

"You're in town? At ten after two in the morning, you're in town? Go, for crissakes, home, Katey. Get some sleep. Call me in the morning."

"Don't hang up."

"Where did you say you were?"

"Didn't."

"Oh, you're a nasty little number, you are," he said, and right then was my chance. To hang up and run.

"What are you wearing?"

"Why?" I'm telling you I *know* what's coming. We've even talked about one day this is what we're going to do, and I still don't run. . . . I am going through some kind of awful fire and brimstone BE-CAUSE I WANT TO!

"Just tell me."

"Come on, Tony," I say, staying. Trembling.

"Look, you called me. You woke me up. You put

me down for boring you with my strudels, as you call them."

"It's not a question of putting you down."

"And you still didn't tell me what you're wearing."

"What's the difference? . . ." EXCEPT I KNOW. GOD PUNISH ME, I DO KNOW!!

"Zip up or buttons?"

"What I'm wearing?"

"Yeah, babes. Does it, for crissakes, zip up or button?"

"It buttons."

"Well, unbutton it."

"What do you mean—unbutton?"

"You know what I mean. Go on."

I heard him. He's got your number, baby. He can even feel that fast shot of adrenalin when he got that hard edge to his voice. "Unbutton," hell, you knew what he was going to end up saying back when you started in on your temper tantrum.

"I don't hear any action," he said.

"Come on, Tony," I said.

His voice got harder.

"Don't be an idiot." Me.

"Do like I say, Kate, or—"

"I'm doing it." Just the thought of his "or" was enough. Or I'll cut you off? Never again? No. I unbuttoned. Turned my back to the booth door.

"Crook the phone in your shoulder."

"It hurts."

"Do it."

"Okay."

"Now. What have you got on?"

"The shroud."

"That brown rag thing."

"Yeah."

"Well, do it all the way down, then."

"I did."

"How do you feel?"

"Nervous."

"But nice?"

"Damn you!"

"I asked you a question."

"You know how I feel. Go on."

"You know, Mrs. Edwards, you are a fast fuck. Fastest around."

"Shut up."

"Where's your right hand?"

"Jesus, Tony—"

"Tell me."

"Okay."

"So I can have you do it again tomorrow. In front of a mirror."

"Tony, this is sick. Sickest thing I ever heard of. You are, we are. Tony, this is weirdo stuff. It's—"

"Tell me what you are doing."

"No."

"I'll tell you. Going round and round, aren't you? Yes, I can see you, pushing up against the cold glass. I know you, baby. Your fist's up you. Up to your wrists, pushing around. Your mouth half open. You know what, you've got a great mouth. Great. I can hear you. Go on. Oh, Jesus. Wake me up every night in the middle of a dream."

And me, far away, moaning for his fantasy. And then Rolf intruding into my what? Superego? The Jiminy Cricket; thou shalt not? Anyway, I couldn't come. Wrong—I could have. I wanted to. Now, as I sit here, goddamn it, I know I wanted to.

I scared myself. Before I turned off I was in the middle, so close to coming, another minute and I'd have split his eardrum with my scream, Oh, God, Rolf, what's wrong with me? I wasn't like this when you married me in my white dimity, a ribbon, for godsake, around my neck, before Christ, my Savior, on my knees, the holes in your shoes forever preserved in our wedding pictures.

Write fast. Think. Get it out. Maybe you'll know. See from a distance where, why you are. Kathy Edwards, you're headed for rapids. You'll lose. Do you want to lose? Is that what you're ultimately looking for? The big, cataclysmic rejection, after all? You're no good. Rolf: asleep at home on your bed, thinking you're there, when you're here, in a public phone booth, unbuttoned, leaning against the wall, your thighs clenched in a death grip, your breasts spread-eagled against the wall, each nipple pressed in a different direction, you're sick, Edwards. Sick, and it's true what men say, that women are the source of all evil, the carriers of lust, the possessors of the strayed paths.

"Did you?"

Tony. I was living four, six, eleven realities at the same moment. Knowing my duties toward him, my lover. Hadn't I called him? I owed him, all right. He was doing me a favor by having me. It was up to me to fulfill and fulfill again. If he wanted me to do it in front of a mirror, did I have a choice?

"What are you doing now?" and I heard myself laugh. Saw myself arrested for indecent exposure over the telephone.

Casual sex is so easy to say, so hard to live with.

What am I doing?

I am committing suicide. What do you think I'm doing?

ANTONY
February 13

What hath God wrought?

With the benefit of technology, Kate and I screwed our brains out over thirty-two miles of rubber-wrapped wire. I came over the phone cord. It was infinitely better than my afternoon "strudel."

What the hell does Kate want from me?

KATHERINE
February 13

I sit here because if I get up the nervous breakdown I'm having will end in a brown paper bag. I really will, tear-soaked and shivering, shatter. It's still raining and the wet sun is going down somewhere else. I have to get up. Rolf will want dinner. He'll be home soon and probably mad at me for something, and it won't be because of Tony he'll be mad.

The cuckolding of Rolf Edwards

Bad woman from the gitgo.
Good woman gone bad.
A mad. A man?
To punish you.
For something to do.
BECAUSE I NEED IT!

Because I'm dying here, not knowing which way to turn. Path to take. (Once taken, took forever?) Am I screwing this stranger because I'm ready to move on? Away? And can't do it alone?

I am in anguish Monday to Friday but with ball-bearing smoothness up comes breakfast, lunch, dinner, Morning, Afternoon, martini with an olive, straight up. . . . My life is tripping its own fantastic with no particular say-so from me.

I do not understand what I am doing!
Shouldn't I?
I hold my lover in my arms, I tell him I love him in

my head. I am here when my husband comes home for dinner because he seems to want me to be here.

I am sleepwalking through my life.

ANTONY
February 18

Oh, my lovely, funny Kate. How I love to be with you. In every way. Every way.

Today: Kate excuses herself from the work table, minces to the kitchen and returns starkers. Then she proceeds to climb onto the table, jut out a hip, and run her hands in her hair.

"Who am I?" she asks.

"Carmen Miranda?"

"No, no. Just a minute." She puffs out her belly.

"Mia Farrow in *Rosemary's Baby?*"

"No dummy." She fluffs around with her tits. "Use your imagination."

"Eleanor Roosevelt?"

"Closer."

"Franklin Roosevelt?"

"You lose."

"Who was it?"

"Your sister-in-law." Whom she's never seen.

She climbs off the table and I climb on, pulling off my shirt and my shoes and whipping my pecker out of my pants. Then I give Kate my back and do a slow grind.

"I know, I know," she giggles, "Brando in *Last Tango.*"

"Right."

Next, Kate does *Winged Victory*. I do Michelangelo's *David*. Then Kate does a pretzel. I do a mushroom. Kate does me picking my nose. I do Kate having an orgasm. Kate does me doing her having an orgasm.

Later, mid-lovemaking, she insists on doing an impression of me fucking. I do her. We continue fucking, playing each other. Flip, flop, we proved beyond any shadow of a doubt that we two are perfectly interchangeable.

Afterward, I squirmed into Kate's panties and bra, sweater and skirt (unzipped). She donned my jockeys and slacks and work shirt. Not one giggle is allowed.

"That was lovely, Tony," I say.

"You weren't bad yourself, Kate," says Kate. "Hungry?"

We have soup and bologna sandwiches and discuss our work.

"We need a stronger conflict between John D. and Rocky, don't you think, Kate?" Kate says.

"Oh, Tony," I say. "You plot like a TV writer."

Nonchalant, we go on like this for an hour.

And then.

Then I stack the dishes in the sink, pick up the books, and head for the door.

"Rolf will be waiting," I say and start for her car.

"Not funny," says Kate, scrambling out of my togs.

"Why not?" I say. "Maybe Rolf won't be able to tell the difference between us, either."

"You dumb bastard!"

I must have hit on a touchy subject.

Moments later, all laughs and love again. At the door to her car, she lifts her skirt and drops her pants, showing me her lovely bottom. "Who am I?" she calls to me.

"I give up."

"Katey Edwards," she calls back and hops into the car without pulling her panties back up.

KATHERINE
February 20

Technological advances are for:

      sitting on
      balancing on
      coming to

As they hum inside you like some mystery sound off an old-time radio show.

No philosophy. No pain. No problems. I did it, I got it, and then I went to my lover's and he plugged me in. I can see very clearly now that I've made my mind up to try it all. As long as I'm at it (there's an expression for this, can't remember it. As long as you're going to make grand larceny, make it worthwhile. Is that it?)

It was not for me. I can't take anything that wild. That beyond—good. That unabashedly hedonist. That bad I must shy from—to retain some kind of equilibrium.

ANTONY
February 20

Today Katey brought an electric typewriter and an electric vibrator. I told her she was overimpressed with technology. She told me she was an efficiency expert.

She masturbated in front of a mirror with the vibrator while I watched her. I had to promise not to touch her. I kept my promise.

I asked her if all the paraphernalia was part of a depersonalizing program. She told me she does not have

77

any program. I told her she was important to me. She
smiled sweetly.

I am sure I am some sort of an experiment for Kate,
or perhaps a bit of therapy. That's okay. Everything's
okay.

While she was in front of the mirror, my vision
slipped gears for a moment and I was watching myself
as her and felt myself coming as she came.

The woman has peculiar ways of getting inside me.

KATHERINE
February 21

It's not stopping, and I'm changing. I am. I even
look different. The men see it, walking down the street,
getting my tires rotated. They know who I am.

ANTONY
February 22

In college, Ted was already a confirmed stoic and
used to lecture me on it. Before he had ever screwed,
he had it all worked out: "Tension and release, tension
and release. There's got to be something better than
that, Tony. You're doomed to become a Sisyphus of
the bedchamber."

I used to argue that the only alternative was boredom.

He used to argue that the only alternative was transcendence.

Well, today Ted has a religious wife and a seductive
secretary and he admits he hasn't had a glimpse of
transcendence since he gave up LSD. And me? I've got
Randy Katey, old Mrs. Tension-and-Release herself,

and I've been longing a lot for boredom lately. Domestic boredom. I could even go for a religious wife today, so I could zero in on the ups and downs of family life for a change instead of the ups and downs of my pecker. Perversion's just another word for nothing else to do. I'm tired of playing the macho alternative to domestic bliss for these late bloomers. I'm tired of all these *Last Tango* tangles. I want to be Dagwood Bumstead for a change. Or Fred MacMurray. I want kids hopping on my shoulders and milk bills to meet and stews on the range and handholding in front of Kung Fu and private jokes that go on for decades and I want to watch one ass grow fat by millimeters instead of watching them change size each month when a new one graces my sheets. If a little purity and continuity means boredom and dreariness, I'll take it.

And, goddamn it, Kate, you're a fool not to take it yourself. You're a sinner for mixing me up in your pretty life, because it IS pretty. A lot prettier than those games of long-distance orgasm. It's all tension and release, baby. All up and down and in and out. Who gave quiet desperation a bad name? Emerson? Bobby Dylan? Well, fuck 'em, Dagwood Bumstead knows more about the meaning of life than either of them.

I am definitely not getting what I want.

I am living out a role I don't believe in anymore.

And it's funny; the only person I can think of to tell about it is old Katey herself.

KATHERINE
February 28, wherein TIME MARCHES ON. (I am not the woman I wuz.)

Rolf's birthday. (A disaster.)
Anecdotes, happenings. An escalation.
My husband has aged another year. We are still married. We go through the ritual of Rolf's birthday. I

am told by my husband that the sign of the Pisces is
the fish. No, I am not told, Christa is. But we both
know already. I suspect that he's had a few before
coming home. I also suspect that Christa suspects. I try
to touch his arm, and mouth "I love you" at him
across the table, but he resists both. I find myself
shrugging internal shoulders. He continues the saga of
the Pisces person.

He tells us that all geniuses including Picasso are
Pisces. That not only is the Piscines a fish but that the
salmon swims upstream against all odds. (He looks at
me and I smile. It is not the reaction he wants. He ex-
pects some other kind of recognition from me, but
when I say in the quiet of the evening, "What's the
matter, honey?" he won't answer me.)

We have a very fine dinner, I think. I have worked
hard. He eats, but like my mother would say, he
doesn't REALLY eat. Okay. Never mind. He then goes on
to remind me, as he has reminded me every single soli-
tary February we have known each other (a very long
time), that had he been born eleven minutes later, I
might have been married to a nine-year-old. He laughs,
Christa's again confused, and I have lived it all before
too many times.

He's angry with me. He's deliberately not enjoying
himself. He's deliberately telling me the same jokes because he knows it irritates me. And I know he doesn't
know about Tony. That THAT'S NOT IT!

I let myself fade out for a few minutes. It's okay, he
has to explain about February 29 again. About being
nine, for Chris again. I have a little time. I force myself
to find out, am I? Probing enough? Really doing all
there is to find out what it is. What is eating him so
much he has to have a few before his own birthday
party?

Remember, kiddo—artists live in garrets alone! So it
doesn't really matter if there's another reason, too.
That one is always available. He'd rather be Picasso

swimming up the Allagash than eating his wife's veal scallopini on a birthday that only pushes him further and further toward the end of what has come to be known in men as "The Prime of Life."

(In women it's called: "The Woman Over Thirty-five.")

And I don't blame him. Who wouldn't rather be Picasso?

"I love you," I say to him again without saying it loud enough for either of them to hear. "I'll make it up to you, this marriage business. If you'll only gimme a chance."

But then Chris gets the joke about Leap Year. They're both laughing because that would make her father three years younger than she is. They're both beginning to relax a little.

Chris bought him a new set of batteries and six tapes for his cassette. I've bought him a book. He's going to love Chris's present. I knew before I paid the $12.95 mine was a mistake.

"Open the presents. Open the presents," Christa's screaming, and I watch her throw her pretty young body into his open arms. I watch the two of them dissolve into each other. And I want to point out to him that artists in garrets don't get to have that kind of arms around their necks either.

"I'm sorry," I think I see him mouth to me over Chris's neck, and suddenly I would do anything in the world to be able to change my present. "I'm sorry," and he's reaching out a hand to include me in their circle. Except I don't really feel out of it and he's not really sorry. He's just separate, that's what he is. He's able to reach out a hand to bring me into a situation that includes Chris but not when it's just him. When it's just him, I'm on permanent bench duty.

Dear Peggy Lee: Is that all there is?

FLASHBACK: Late afternoon. Small town. Rain. Small woman in rubber boots and slicker scurries through downpour. In a big hurry. Going nowhere. Passes bookstore. Looks in window. Sees book. Stops in same big hurry. Enters bookstore. Touches book. Flips pages. Lifts book. Woman's face looks spattered with tears. It's really rain. Same difference.

Woman ponders price of book. Turns to page 81 and studies drawing of man on all fours bearing woman. Turns to page 83 and studies colored print of man giving finger to woman with her own up her own whatsis.

It is woman's husband's birthday.

Book is present.

Book is *Joy of Sex*.

Book is mistake.

A cataclysm.

A Black Day at Bad Book.

Only why a personal affront? All I thought was, Gee, what a lot of good, clean, American fun, "the first real adult sex information book ever published." I thought maybe we could pray for rain and send Chris out to a double-feature and three boxes of popcorn.

He called me, an ad for *New York* magazine and we were off—

"I've lost sight," he said, and I don't know where I'm going. And if I didn't like who he was and what he stood for I could always move out smartly, he'd try to be regular with the alimony payments.

"Alimony?"

"Well, I really think you're going flippo on me, every day a new Barnum and Bailey freak show."

"You're going to divorce me over a cookbook?"

"We are mismated, you and I."

"So what? It's kept us going for fifteen years; don't knock it."

"It's too late for Road to Lifeisms."

I touch his leg. He brushes off my hand and shrugs. I touch it again. This time he shakes his head.

"Real life, my dear, has very little to do with all

your celebrated celebrating," he says with the breath of North Wind between us. "Real life has to do with staying above water."

End of birthday party—renewal of crisis.

ANTONY
March 1

The radio was playing "Deep Purple" when Kate scampered in today. She dropped her books and we danced.

We danced for two hours.

I am a teenager in love.

KATHERINE
March 3

Angie called. High. On herself. She's riding for a big fall but in the meantime is screwing everything in sight.

Why is it I think she'll fall? Because what's that high must come down and at that pace it can't be gradual.

Angie, you're hysterical, remember when it used to be trading cards? You're no different, buddie. You had to have them all, too. EVERY horse ever printed, EVERY scene, EVERY allover pattern, EVERY famous painting, EVERY flower arrangement even if you didn't like it, if it weren't worth anything, if you couldn't stand to look at it, just as long as it was there, Angie baby. . . .

And if you want my opinion, I wouldn't be surprised if you had orgasm problems. Anybody who has to screw THAT much has to be proving SOMETHING!

She also said she thinks Rolf's lost his gallery.

I think maybe that's it. I also think why didn't I think of that? But why Rolf doesn't tell me . . . ?

I go back over the months. I remember the time when I tried to rub his neck and he pulled away. When I said, "Let's take a walk, and hold hands, and share each other's secrets just like yesterday," and he wouldn't.

This isn't *Joy of Sex* I'm talking about, baby; this is, keep me company while I take a bath, clean the kitchen, polish your shoes. This is day to day, Rolf— I'm floating out to sea. Don't you care? Why won't you talk to me?

KATHERINE
March 4

Angie was right. He did lose the gallery. I called Edmund. Rolf'd gone ahead and sold the damn pink and blue out of the studio. Without giving Edmund his cut. I told him not to. I told him, I told him.

Unwritten rule of the galleries: Never, but never sell even a single black line on a single white piece of paper without giving your gallery dealer his third.

Never.

Never.

They'll find out and kick your ass.

Into the street, Rolf, except who pays any attention to a nagging wife? Now I'm really a traitor. Loving somebody else while my husband's down, and out of his gallery like a newcomer.

No wonder you've been sulking through my life like the Loch Ness Monster, you big boob.

Goddamn it, I told you not to!!!!!! !!!!!!

Ralph, a throwback to my game-show days, called
this morning. He wanted to know if I'd like to do some
off-the-books quiz question writing. God knows, I
could use the money, but I told him I was wrapped up
in a new project. Oh, yes, I am wrapped up!

Ralph related the following story: One day he came
home from shooting three back-to-back shows and his
little boy (four, I think) asked him, "Daddy, are we
live or on tape?"

That's today's question, Kate: Is this thing we have
live or on tape? The reason I ask, my friend, is because
I keep getting the spooky feeling that there is something once removed about our little affair. (Did I say
"affair"? Forgive me, our little "physical understanding." Better?) Not that we're repeating ourselves—at
least I can vouch that we are unique in the Amato an-
nals. And practiced as you seem, I do not get the
feeling that I am seventh in a series for you. No, it's
something else. It's the way we anticipate each other.
You give me a lingering case of déjà vu.

Today Kate came a half hour early. She came
equipped with file cards, clipboard, a volume called
Liquid Gold, another called *Wheels,* and a third called
Joy of Sex. I looked them over in order while she
made espresso. (Kate needs coffee like the sun needs
kindling.)

Liquid Gold is a rare find, an encyclopedic compen-
dium of the petrol industry up to 1939, the year it was
published and presumably the year it went out of print.
The pages are as flaky as a baklava. It gave me the
chills; 1939 is the year of my birth— Am I getting
flaky, too?

Wheels is a potboiler about a *rubber* dynasty. God help us, it is one of our models. It reminds me of quiz shows, with its boring details. I remember Ralph's first rule for a good quiz format: make the viewer think she's learning something so she won't feel guilty about frittering away a half hour.

Joy of Sex is in mint condition with its glossy *Saturday Evening Post* pictures of cocks and cunts. Same rule as Ralph's: make the reader think she's learning something so she won't feel guilty, etc. Lenny Bruce would have loved this one; if they had called it *Joy of Fucking,* it wouldn't have made it past the front door of Brentano's. . . . But what's this I see scratched on the frontleaf in Kate's inimitable hand? The following message: "Since you've let your *Art in America* subscription lapse, I thought we'd try something new. Happy Birthday, Katey."

This little greeting was not written for me.

But what the hell?

An hour with *Liquid Gold,* one with *Wheels,* and yet another with *Joy.* ("Let's spread Joy," as Rocco used to say whenever she walked by our corner.) And so we did.

Kate's idea is to use it like the *I Ching:* open a page at random and do it by the book. Today we did something called "Pinning the Butterfly." I was the lepidopterist.

See what I mean? Always a touch of the game. Are we live or on tape, Kate? Huh? When we're trembling with it, when you're digging your nails into my ass and whimpering, when you're pounding the bed and screaming, "Oh, God, Tony"—when we come so hard we're almost retching, is it all just fun and games???

It can't be! CANNOT!

Ordinary people don't do it like this, my friend. Believe me. There is fucking and there is fucking. This is something else. (Oh, shit, do I sound like Gene and Marsha with their "really fucking"?)

and fucking. We can't keep them neat and separate
anymore.

Me: Okay. It's all right with me. Really.

Kate: Don't say that.

Me: Okay.

Kate: Hold me, Tony.

Me: I am.

I think we held each other, standing there in the
doorway, for about a half hour. Something like a half
hour. And not talking. Just shivering. Shivering and
tingling. I wish I could get a handle on what it was that
was happening. It happened last night, this morning,
those sudden embraces from out of nowhere. Hugs that
contacted each other everywhere. Not sex. I mean not
prick-cunt, slam-fondle sex. Something sexier than sex.
Something sharp and fully awake. Something like sniffing cocaine or passing out. Something like coming from
the tips of everything in me.

I am one thing when I hold Kate like that. I am one
beautiful thing. And so is she.

KATHERINE
March 10

I know something Tony doesn't. That's why he's
whole and I'm shredded. Top Secret. A mind divided
against itself. No, not a mind; I've deliberately turned
that part off. These several days are not to be smothered by thought and consequences and betrayals. They
are a soul sauna. And I need them.

The high. The sweets. I'm going to concentrate on
knowing that Tony's writing, too, not the book, but
about us. He said he was going to lie down, but I just
know that's what he's doing. And I want to look to see
what he's saying, but couldn't. I've always known I'd
look at anybody's diary. . . . But not his. His is as

sacred as mine. Respect? Or just fear. Repercussions?
And don't say love. It isn't love, I swear.

Except it feels like it. Especially when I close my
eyes and forget who's supposed to be there when I
open them.

Tony.

It's nice with Tony. It's easy. It's so easy with Tony;
help me. What if I make that one final mistake? Take
sides. And find out in the morning I've pulled the hem-
lock after all.

Tony.

The second Razaumovsky and Tony. By Hamilton
Falls and Tony. Oh, God, maybe it isn't love, but I
swear to you it feels like it.

Usually music interferes. With Rolf it does. I begin
listening, but with Tony nothing interferes, I'm just
wholly taken up. (But does that mean it's purely simple
escapism or is that the way it's supposed to be; speak of
authority figures and other devils. . . . The way it's
supposed to be! Hah.) Except it was purely exhausting
and purely like a romantic novel: Where they call it
commingling. Cause that's what we were doing, Tony
and I, the two of us out of our minds with a commingling of pain and delirious perfection. Crying sexual
pain, screaming out as if wounded. Just thinking of it
and I'm high. I bit him and didn't even know it. As
good as Beethoven, I swear, those four strings between
sensation and nothingness. You can't believe it's only
your body. Your body which you love and run your
hands over to adore it. Oh, Tony, Tony, just the sound
of you on me, in me!! If I die now I won't need ex-
treme unction. I am purified, love or no love. I can't
believe it. The water so cold and crystal, the music, us,
the feel. Enough. We're going to climb the hill behind
Hamilton. I'm going to see him again, feel him. I can't
believe it. And crying again, of course. I keep crying.
Why the hell do I keep crying?

ANTONY
March 10

Sitting on a rock below Hamilton Falls, high on its white sound drumming us like a mantra. We are not touching. We are not looking at each other. It is Saturday afternoon, roughly four years after last night.

A minute ago:

Kate: Okay, Tony. Who are we?

Me: Dagos. Simple wops. Coming home at last.

Kate: Defrocked Sicilian peasants.

Me: Yup. Who took a wrong turn about a century ago.

Kate: We don't belong here.

Me: I know. I knew it when I put on a pair of white bucks in high school. I said, "That's not you, Tony. You're a fraud. You're a shepherd. Or a café keeper. Not this."

Kate: I am your wife. Your sister.

Me: I know.

Kate: Should we talk about what is wrong with this now?

Me: No. Please. Not yet.

Kate: We have to.

Me: Not yet.

Kate: Okay.

KATHERINE
March 11

"Then," I told him, "then it was unlike anything before or since." "Then" about Rolf and me. Meeting on a shoestring, living on short ribs. And the more I told about it, the more ambiguous I felt.

(That's what I'm trying to wrestle out of me: Which is stronger, Katherine Edwards? Which? Think! *This* could be it! The desire to turn traitor with this warm, deep-rooted pizza I'm baking myself into, or to keep certain memories sacred with secrecy? I mean, doesn't Rolf deserve any ironclad inviolability? Yes, I scream to myself, calling myself a bitch, of course he does, that part of you that loves that part of Rolf and you that no one, not even someone named Tony, could ever put asunder!

So why am I telling him?

Sitting under the spring breezes from Keats and Byron and cherry orchards and Scudahoo Seudahay, oh, Rolf, I can't believe what's happening to me. When are you going to get the hook and drag me off this stage??????

Stop me before I say more? Before there's no going home again?

And what else? Did I leave out anything?

About Antoinette? Mary? Sister Margaret? The boys? I doubt it. Even about peeking at Mike through the keyhole, trying to see up his wee-wee to where it came from. Getting him to whack it big and scary. Rolf, that I never even told you, because it belonged to Mike and wasn't mine to share like a piece of Butterfinger.

I also told him about the time I almost died from what they thought was diptheria but turned out to be a high fever of unknown origin, and how Mama repeated that phrase over and over as if I'd won first prize in the spelling bee.

Told him? I dredged up parts of me I'd thought had long since gone to rot.

For instance, First Communion, which I'd never have been able to tell Rolf, because WASPs don't get confirmed in white satin when God is still a Savior in a nest of vanilla cloud, on the back of every redwing blackbird. WASPs don't have any idea what white satin feels like against seven-year-old skin. Especially Rolf, whose mother left the Lutherans to go Unitarian. A Unitarian is a mortal sin worse than brajole on Friday. We never talk about Rolf's mother. Whereas Tony is different. The skinny kid in the skinned knees who knelt next to me, his tongue as pink as mine waiting for the wafer. See Rolf on Religion, last year or year before. Rolf is funny on religion, he makes me pee. Rolf can be very funny. Never mind . . .

Home is where the roots are. Yes, *Tony is home.*

Why does everything that finally works out, work out too late?

Typical Catholic guilt syndrome, no? "If it's right, God will find a way." That's what Mama would have said. The other side of the same communion wafer, only I seemed to have inherited only the hell's fire and brimstone side. Oh, how I wailed. I loved, ergo everything connected to me and mine was doomed. My husband and child would have an accident on the way home, the school would know how to tell me, I would go into an immediate catalepsy, I would . . . Bull, bull, bull, I told myself. Listen, Tony, your Love, he's talking. He was . . . a blue streak, but I didn't hear a word, only ran my fingers around his temples and swallowed his look (our look). I smiled through my tears, as they say. I adored him without having to listen. What did it matter what the details were, I had him here, right next to my corruption. My guilt, joy, my tears, my confusion, and my love, all mixed up, marinara.

ANTONY
March 11

Last night; Kate and me in the kitchen creating a new spaghetti sauce. I am slicing up carrots.

Kate: No carrots, Tony.

Me: Of course, carrots. For texture.

Kate: No carrots. I insist, no carrots.

Me: Not just texture. Vitamins. This is a health spaghetti.

Kate: What kind of an Italian are you? There is no such thing as a health spaghetti. We thrive on deficiencies.

Me: Carrots. Carrots. Carrots.

Kate: Not carrots.

Carrots are now flying around. And sliced onions. Peppers. Tomato paste smeared on our faces, our arms. Our clothes are coming off. A carrot is slipping up my . . .

KATHERINE
March 11

. . . Soft, mushy tomato sauce. Into my Ship 'N Shore. Into my wraparound, which he soon unwrapped. Into my dollar-ninety-five cents bikinis. Mushy, gooshy tomato sauce, all warm, all sticky. Under and into—

"Needs a little more garlic," laughing and oozing myself around on the floor, Tony on top of me, eating himself down to my slithering naked self.

And then pasta, pounds of it, scooped into and out of me, sliding on it, slurping it. It was disgusting. It was fantastic. I rolled myself out of everything else I

still had on and then around on the floor again, this
time into the cheese sauce we'd toppled on top of the
tomatoes. We both rolled in it. We both ate our sup-
pers off each other. He sucked egg noodles out from
between my toes. I nibbled on watercress and Spanish
onion out of his. "You are the best cook ever"—Me.

"Sssshhh, stupid, just eat"—Him. "Think of the
starving Armenians."

ANTONY
March 12

. . . Last night: Watching the "Starlight Movie"
double feature, naked, wrapped together in a blanket.

Me: This is the best movie I ever saw. (It is a film
about the invasion of giant grasshoppers.)

Scene: "Starlight" second feature (Dean Martin a
drunken cowboy; John Wayne saves him).

Kate: Can I suck you?

Me: Okay. But it's going to be a limp spaghetti for a
while longer yet.

Kate: I know. I like it that way. I love your dick.

Me: Even like this?

Kate: YUP. Me and it have a thing going. An understanding.

Me: oh, God . . . Is it possible to come without an
erection?

Kate: (Mumble.)

Me: What?

Kate: I can't hear you. . . . There's a prick in my
mouth.

More. A thousand. More. More events, feelings,
thoughts in those forty-eight hours than in my life to
date. From out of nowhere. From out of crazy Kate.

KATHERINE
March 12—pitch-black middle of the night

Dear Diary, Old Friend. No complications. A simple, to-the-point statement. I am a happy woman. I woke up with my hand underneath Tony Amato's ass, and outside the stars didn't give a damn, bright as anything. I didn't look for a deep, meaningful dialogue with myself. I didn't look for anything and nothing came. Nothing but quiet, gentle serenity. God bless me, I must be in love. My other-world responsibilities aren't under the bed or in the closet.

Called Angela.

"Mrrrnnnngngginng," or a resonable facsimile, she said, "Wussmittr," and before I could tell her I'm in love, what am I going to do? she said, "Goddammit, I did it again."

"Angie?"

Awake. Giggling and I was sorry I called.

"It's better than stealing a Halston," she said. She better watch out. Marshall Fields caught her in Chicago and threatened to wire her boss and she had diarrhea for three months.

"Listen Ange, you're . . ."

"No, I'm telling you, Breakfast of Champions is nothing compared to me."

"Angie."

"Kathy, take it from me. Even too much isn't enough; you're crazy to settle so easily. Mad out of your mind."

"Who with now?" I asked her, but already had my ears shut. Don't tell me, Angie, don't tell me, you're scaring me. You're souring my sweet time and taking the skim off my butterscotch pudding. I'm not like THAT, Angie—can't even you understand? I called up

98

to talk about moon-June-bloom/tea for Tony and me/ cots by the sea and end up finding out. If me and Angie aren't the good girls, from the nice families, who went to church and knew their catechism by heart, where are they? And what chance do any of us have?

And worse.

Worse because, NO, Angie Boutis, you have for the first time in my life let me down. I don't want to talk about "doing it," Angie. . . . What is this thing called love? That's what I called to talk about. Love, Angie, am I in it? I came to you for answers. But this time all I got was another chapter in shoplifting. What do I do now? Ask Tony?

ANTONY
March 13

She left last night. Under protest. Despite pleas. What could she do? What can I do? I am—I have been since she left—desolate. I have never felt so connected as with Katey, never so alienated as without her. So empty. So in need of completion.

I have to do something. I am dizzy. I never expected this. I have no plans, no rehearsals to cover it. Katey and I are unique for me.

I don't know how this happened. It was not simply a dreamy weekend. I know. I am an expert on dreamy weekends. I am an expert on everything except love.

KATHERINE
March 13

THE INEVITABLE—or, the Hare and the Tortoise Confront Cocks at Finish Line.

I AM THE FINISH LINE—or, Talk About Dirty
Seconds!!!!!!!

Instinct. Terror. Discovery?

I came home, dripping with guilt; I am not by
nature a deceiver. I do not lie at will. I came home, diaphragm thick with various varieties of goo—Tony's,
Ortho's, and mine—in place. I came home worn, sore,
and glowing with contentment first, unwieldy anxiety
second, and third. Bases overloaded. I came home to
sink into the Sealy and dream of the afterglow, but
when I came home, Rolf wanted to do it.

He knows! was my first reaction. My first reaction
was not, well, he's human . . . sure he wants to. No, I
suppose I no longer think of Rolf wanting anything
from me.

He'll feel it was my second reaction. The wet plug.
He'll know I did it. He'll smell it on me. He'll know!!!

"Just a minute," I whisper, straining toward the
bathroom door, for the first time in too long, Rolf
breathing down my tonsils.

"What's the hurry?" he wants to know, his fingers
going up the tunnel, two by fist. "There's plenty of
time," he tells me, licking the places on my neck that
are already coated with salt. "You taste good," he tells
me. He rubs his palm over my sleeping nipples. "You
feel good, you've got on too many clothes . . . you've
got plenty of time."

He's in the mood for a long, slow siege. He will
count. I will be played like an Amati, every harmonic
attended to. He has had a weekend of adoration, he
has had a weekend of success sans surcease, he has
had a surfeit of selfishness, and tonight he is taking me
off the diet he has been keeping me on. Tonight I am
to reap *les richesse*. While I vacillate between fear of
discovery and fear of insufficiency. I have already come
beaucoup times today. I do not think my doer down

there is up for any more than recovering. I am done in.

I must also get to the john to cover myself. He must hear the running water. He must know that when and if he feels rubber, it is there for him, and yet he repeats, "Not yet," and forces my thighs apart with his knees. He wants to look down and watch that special schizophrenia spread across my eyes. He wants to hold back and begin a last-minute marathon.

"Come," he commands, his hands holding mine, his thwump thwumping me.

"Too chancy," I beg. "Lemme at least up, Rolf, come on, you never know, one drop is more than all it takes. . . . Please!!!" Terror, and then, after one more hesitation he does, he wonders? No, he slides off enough so that I slip through, into the sanctity of the bathroom where, while the water runs, I think dirty thoughts, run my mind down the pages of *My Secret Garden,* and come back ready for the siege of Thermopylae pass.

And pass. With a surprise of cache of three. Three hard-won head-splitters, the last coordinated on Rolf's dime, the two of us wrapped around each other as if for all the world we were in love.

But who is the real and undisputed winner, finally? The tortoise to whom I am by law property? Or my ravenous rabbit, quick over me, through McGregor's lettuce patch?

The turtle languishes over my topside, luxuriating in belly swells and tit tops. He has a fatter, somnambulant tongue that licks you into a deep sweat. He breathes hot, tickling air over your surface. He takes your time and his. He wins by innuendo.

The hare harasses. He whispers fast, right away, from the start, "Lemme in," and settles back for combustion action. Faster and faster, charging your nether atmosphere by demands unyielding. The hare had no time for slower motion. He sees the finish line from the first. He wins by blocking all the exits.

The turtle touches old, hidden caches, long since larded with booty.

The hare has no truck with primrose paths. He pinches you to attention. He has come to come.

This turtle, bringing forth a sleeping beauty.

I know before my last eruption I am running a fever. As predictable as history. I get sick when too much is at stake.

What's at stake?

Me. The flames already up to my crotch.

ANTONY
March 14

If this isn't love, I am Nelson Rockefeller. And if I never have a cent, I'll be as rich as.

ANTONY
March 15

Have any of those endocrinologists who are all the vogue done experiments with people who are in love?

I volunteer.

Obviously, something inside is secreting like mad these days, squirting drops of GL-99, or whatever, into my bloodstream. Potent stuff, GL-99. Takes getting used to. Should never take it when tightrope walking. Now, if they could isolate the stuff, and put it in our reservoirs, we'd have world peace in minutes flat. Put the Maharishi out of business.

Aha, but put an overload on private eyes. Infidelity would be rampant. Innocent housewives would be falling head over heels for errant TV writers.

Maybe it's not such a good idea.

KATHERINE
March 16

Lost track of days. Mon., Tues., Wed., . . . don't remember. Stayed in bed. Slept most of the time. Tony called a lot. I won't answer.

"Tell him I'm sick."

"Tell him I'll call back when I get better." Whenever I get better. If I get better.

(Fantasies of dying. Fantasies of everybody crying. Who cries the most, King Solomon? Who is the one who really loves? Who will suffer when I'm gone? Who can't get along without me?)

Rolf coming in, Can he do anything for me? Rolf looking at me from doorway. "Poor baby," Rolf saying. Rolf responding to the Me-helpless. Always there when I'm on my back. It was only the demanding "I need it" he shrank from. I couldn't look at him. I turned my face to the wall and let the fever swallow me.

ANTONY
March 17

Called Kate today. She can't get away for a few more days. She said something about our having to keep up with our work, no matter what else is happening. I told her I needed her. She said she needed me. That was it. There was nothing more to say.

I called her a second time a few minutes later to inform her that I loved her madly. I am shameless. I also seem to be a bit humorless these days. Humorless but happy. I guess that is possible. Humorless because this thing is no joke. Happy because this thing is no joke.

KATHERINE
March 18

I was born, I grew up, I fell in love, I fell out of love. I fell in, I fell out of love several, many, all the time more times. I met Rolf. He wiped all the tears away. Rolf put his shoulders between me and the world. Rolf made it all better. I married Rolf. I had a son with Rolf. The son got meningitis. I had a daughter with Rolf. We named her after his rich Aunt Christina. We call her Chris. When his rich Aunt Christina died, it turned out she had her own daughter, unbeknownst to the rest of the family. Her name was Betty and inherited Chris's inheritance. We got older. So now I'm in love? Does that statement fit any of the others? There is no continuum to that statement. I've already been in love. You don't just break up a continuum because you're in love. But I am in love, I feel him when he's in the room, know when he'll laugh. I sense his arm next to mine. The hairs on my legs stand up. Am I Anna Karenina? To throw myself under the cowcatcher of the B & O?

He wants me to leave my husband.

Do I want to leave my husband?

Leave my husband? My husband is the man I married and lie next to, fix Spam for, smell in my sleep, know so well. You don't leave these knowledges. It's like leaving the odor you yourself leave on a wool dress. There is no such leaving. It is yours irrevocably.

Tony: What do you mean irrevocably? People get divorced every day. The entire economy of Haiti is based on people leaving each other. How can you grab me to your breast the way you grab and talk about irrevocably?

You are joshing yourself, Katherine Edwards. Joshing Us!

I am shitting myself. I am not joshing myself. I am irrevocable. I am not irrevocable. I have 103 fever, I don't have 103 fever . . . or is that just the leftover from a perpetual Chinese dinner squeezing my brain together? Or a tumor? Or a middle-aged migraine? Or . . . God, Tony, give me some room. Let me think about it. I just never thought about it before. I never, can't you understand that, ever, ever, ever, ever, ever gave it a thought!!!!!!!

ANTONY
March 19

Called Kate. She was distant, matter-of-fact. It took me the longest time to figure out that Rolf must have been there. I told her I loved her as he hovered over her. She said, "No, I don't think we can use that. Look at your notes on the Aga Khan."

To which I replied: "I want to be deep inside you right now."

To which she replied: "Okay . . . I'll call you tomorrow."

Does she still fuck him? Oh, God, I can't think about it.

Two months ago, I was sure he was not a cuckold because he was beyond that. Today I am sure I am a cuckold.

I must work. Something. I am fluctuating between total emptiness and total submersion in Kate.

I have to think about all this soon. But not yet. I am too disoriented. I have no sense of my future.

Trouble in River City and not to do with me. For a distinct change Chris and Rolf are having a few bouts with white water. For probably the first time. I do believe she's discovered the possibility that daddies aren't always perfect and possibly even vice versa. That retreat for Fathers and Kids at least eliminated the middle woman and left the lovebirds with only each other to confront. And dump on.

Interesting.

Chris in *my* skirt, *my* heels, *my* makeup, with *my* bra over *my* sweater.

Altogether cute, I thought.

Altogether a little too enticing, I think Rolf thought.

Him: Why don't you go upstairs and make your bed?

Her: Oh, Daddy.

Him: I mean it; isn't it about time you helped your mother once in a while?

Her: Oh, Daddy. (This time with her eyes to the ceiling like Ben's Angel.)

Him: And get out of those damn shoes before you break your ankle.

For the third time her line was only, "Oh, Daddy," except this time she added May West's swivel and Marilyn's pout: My daughter, the shaving cream commercial . . . and right on target: his; I could see him swallowing his spleen as I left . . . To keep from belting her or what? I wondered.

I didn't stay to find out. Let Lassie come home on her own for a change. As she would. Ultimately. In her sneakers and sweat shirt to sit on Daddy's lap, feed him Black Crows while the two of them watched some distant, safe broad get hers on the telly.

I didn't stay because I had something on my mind. Something that wasn't going away.

DREAM: Me, fighting with it. (That's all.) That's the whole dream. All's who's there is me. All's I'm doing is fighting. Like Joe Louis. With something identified only as IT.

ANTONY
March 21

Katey is a mother.

What a peculiar thought!

A mother. Like Anna is a mother. Like mamma mia is a mamma.

Of course, I know Chris. And I've closely inspected those hairline stretch marks on Katey's belly.

But a mother?

Today, Katey snoozed for a moment after our love, my lips half puckered around her nipple. (How wonderfully salty she is. Salt of the earth. My Nordic confections would taste so bland after a lick at Katey!) And, half asleep, she pulled me closer and whispered, "Chris."

Chris?

I think I shuddered. It had never occurred to me that this little jumping jack of a woman had room in her for mother love, too! And that cunt, gobbling nether-mouth that is for taking, feeding, sucking. It takes in; it does not give out. Katey's cunt is for swallowing me, not for making a baby.

Chris!

What a lonely feeling it gave me. It's lingered all day. How many other things does me lady love? If there's mother love in there, can wifely love be far behind? Does she love her country as well? Her Savior?

I think I have a terminal case of arrested development. At thirty-five, I cannot connect lover and mother. No wonder I didn't stay married.

I didn't say anything to Kate about her little whisper. But I woke her by stuffing her so fully not one maternal thought could leak out. She awoke and came at the same time, then opened her eyes and said, "I love you inside me."

Inside me!

Then that's where I'll stay!

KATHERINE
March 22

Scared. Got home ten minutes before time to pick up Christa. Filthy, dress ripped, sore. Sore all over, sore, my hair sore. He'd pulled it. He'd held me. He'd ripped my skirt up above my pants. He'd dug his knee into my thigh.

"You want it so bad, I'll give it to you."

"Tony, oh, God, Tony, you're hurting me. Tony."

"You think I'm not hurting? Spread your legs. I mean it, I'll . . ."

I looked at him. He pressed down harder on my arms. What was I going to tell Rolf, daring not mention his name, Tony'd gone crazy. I was afraid he really would hurt me, and then he let go. He both fell on me and let go at the same time.

"You're killing me, baby," he moaned into my hair. "I didn't hurt you; tell me I didn't hurt you."

"Tony . . . Tony!" I pressed hair away from his eyes. The sweat. "I know. I know." I sucked tears from his eyes.

"Did I hurt you?"

"Always," I said.

"Never," I said.

"You've got me so crazy I don't know what I'm doing anymore"—Tony, pressing his cheek on the bruise on my thigh.

"Katey, my darling. Listen to me. I need you, Kate."

He looked up with the expression on his face that he'd pulled on his mom. Really. I could see him, five, six years old, short pants, wide, lash-covered eyes. He did need me, so what was I holding out on him for? Didn't I truly understand him?

He was, for a moment, only a moment, piteous, and I couldn't stand it. Piteous was not what I wanted him to be. My husband was piteous. My husband needed me.

"Take me," I cried, wrenching my head from side to side. Yes, I was glad he lay his cheek on my bruised leg, but still I wanted his desire. Not his need. Not all the time, need, need, need. I had enough needs in my life.

"Never mind," I whispered. "Take me, Tony. That's what I *need*. Right now that's all I need."

ANTONY
March 22

A sweet song of an afternoon with Kate. Something new added. Something old gone. Jealousy added, lightheartedness gone.

Mid-lovemaking, the lady remarks that she is worried about what all this will do to her marriage.

Without missing a stroke, I reply that I hope it ruins her marriage.

Thump.

Her marriage is nothing compared to this anyhow.

Thump.

Her marriage was finished when she stepped in the door a few weekends ago.

Thump.

Kate says, Let's talk about it later.

I say, Let's now. You brought it up.

Kate says, Oh, God. Finish me off, you idiot.

I pull out, withdraw, as they say, and remark, "Always time for that. Let's get these family worries out of the way first."

Kate: What in the hell do you think you're doing?

Me: It's called coitus interruptus.

Kate: Well, don't interrupt us, you bastard. Fuck me, love me.

Me: Can't do both at the same time.

Kate: What in hell are you talking about?

Me, out of bed, my pecker bobbing around like a fly rod, "Our fucking days are over, or hadn't you noticed? I love you. I'm going to need you more and more. And you're going to need Rolf less and less."

Kate: Okay, make love to me. Now.

Me: You just want to come.

Kate: You're goddamned right I do.

Me: That's not good enough.

Kate: Why not? I want you to make me come. You. Anthony Aamato. You. Your prick. Your everything. Damn it, Tony, stick it into me. You're killing me.

I do.

She comes.

I come.

Happy, happy. Except I'm worried. I need her.

ANTONY
March 23

Willie back from his travels this evening. He wants to know what I've been eating for breakfast lately and

could he have some. He says he hasn't seen me as
jubilant since the days of *grappa* and LSD.

I tell him what I am eating for breakfast is too salty
for his palate.

I tell him I in love am.

He says tosh to that.

I say I am crazy with it.

How happy I am to see Willie again.

ANTONY
March 24

I have always known Katherine Edwards.
That is a fact.

ANTONY
March 26

I love her too much. I need more of her. I need all
of her. And I cannot have all of her.

She loves me. I am sure of that. It started out as a
game, a release, an out—she's admitted that. No
blame. I've done the same. Worse, much worse.

But now it is altogether a new thing. We are new
people together. That is a fact. We have been trans-
muted. We have been blessed. We know that. We say
it to each other.

And every day she goes home.

HOME!

I hate the word when she says, "I guess I've got to
go home."

THIS IS HOME, KATE! I am your home.

I think I would do anything to have all of her. For
the first time I understand what a crime of passion is.

It's not really passion at all. I can imagine murdering Rolf Edwards coldly, without passion at all. I do not hate him. I do not know him. I simply want to erase him from Kate's life. So we can be happy. It would be a crime of happiness.

I have to be careful. I have to be patient. I do not feel in charge of myself. Losing control is wonderful. And it is horrifying.

I have to sit quietly.

Jesus God, I am crying on the paper.

ANTONY
March 27

This morning I decided to stop seeing Kate. Drop the book, forget everything, get back to normal. Maybe move to the city again. Or Hollywood. Go back to automatic living.

Alone, over coffee, it seemed so clear. I had to do it. Now, before we kill ourselves with it. To save her marriage. To save my sanity.

When she came in the door this afternoon, I knelt in front of her and licked her cunt like a puppy. I told her I would never leave her.

ANTONY
March 30

Oh, Jesus, I'm going off the deep end.

Remember when you had pride, Tony, old friend? The kind that Father Ducessi tried to knock out of you with twenty Our Fathers at a clip? The kind that Dr. Z called my "excessive ego preoccupation"? Well, you'll both be glad to hear that I've been cured in a trice by a demidago whore.

(Forgive me, Kate. You are an angel. I am the whore.)

I could not help myself. This afternoon I asked Kate if she still slept with Rolf.

She said she would rather not talk about it.

I said that just a simple yes or no would do and then I'd drop it.

She said a simple yes.

I did drop it. I asked her how that was possible.

She said it was simply possible and that she would rather not talk about it.

I asked her if it would make things more convenient for her if I moved in with her and Rolf and Chris.

She told me I was crazy.

KATHERINE
April 2

Dear Diary, don't be mad. I couldn't write. I couldn't even sleep. Tony's pulling something. He's, damn him, torturing me. I should be glad. You're supposed to be glad when men fight over you (not that Rolf's exactly putting on the gloves), but besides the regular war of attrition Tony's waging, he's deliberately giving it to me, too . . . or rather not giving it to me. Pulling out just before I come off. Or moving. Or leaning backward, taking his tongue off my breast, easing up . . . He's suddenly found a hundred ways to leave me hanging there. Then he looks at me as if to double dare. Ok, Bitch . . . you want it? Put out. And you know what? . . . Put out your marriage, the bastard. He wants to force me to jump ship. Or he won't let me . . . But I have to . . . You know I have to . . . I'm up all night . . . I'm back in the car screaming

again!!!!! My sweet husband paid for that car. Artists
don't have wives—DAMN you, Tony, my darling. Oh,
God, I need him. Tony, don't do this to me, baby. My
baby, give it, give me time. You have to give me time,
Tony. Tony, fuck me, don't you know I can't think
straight?

ANTONY
April 5

Home to Mommy, Daddy, Aunty, Gramps, Franco,
et al. . . . My family, right or wrong. The Italian-
American alliance. The usual scene. Gramps grumbling
with the "assimilation blues": "Whatsamatter? Nobody, he speak his own tongue no more?" Franco with
Anna, looking forlorn and five years older than me instead of vice versa. That boy is smothered by tits,
smothered by Anna's two big ones. He's taken to winking at me constantly, more conspiratorial than broth-
erly, wants me to know he's getting plenty on the side,
not hedged in by those mammoth mammaries. Momma
wants to know if I'm seeing anybody.

Anna: Tony? Sure. He's seeing *anybody*.

From her mouth, everything sounds obscene.

Poppa: You know, Tony, you made a mistake once.
But that's no reason you shouldn't try again.

Me: I think you're right.

Franco laughs, winks.

I am too old for this, for these visits. And I am
afraid they will make me hate Katey for being Italian.
These visits make me long for all the Annalenas and
Brigits and Irenas of the world. The mindless blondes
who speak from the guttural, who clip their consonants
and their underarm hair, who only scream in their
sleep.

Momma: So you are seeing someone? A nice girl?

For "nice," read "Italian."

Me: I am, it's true. She's very nice. She makes a great fettuccine.

I'm really laying it on. Momma has her arms around me, hands on my ears. "Fettuccine? Really, Tony?"

This kills Franco. For once his nose for double meaning is accurate.

Me: Great fettuccine, Momma. Except, she insists on putting carrots in it.

Poppa: This is serious, Tony?

Momma: You'll bring her home?

Sure, I'll bring her home. Her and Rolf and Christa. I'll bring home my Italian whore and teach everybody a lesson.

Momma: Whatsa trouble, Tony? We aren't good enough? What is she, Roman?

Me: That's it, Mom, Roman. A real snob. But I'm working on her.

Franco can barely contain himself.

Pit stop at Leo's on my way back. I lay a full confession on him. I have a compulsion for confessing to Jews. Makes me feel much cleaner than laying it on some beskirted Irish Father.

Leo finds the whole tale hilarious.

"Ho, ho," says Leo. "Coming home to roost, are you? It's a sign of middle age, you know."

"Leo, you're missing the whole point. She's married. She's married and I'm in love with her."

"Terrific. Perfect. No problems."

"You don't get it, Leo. I love her. Remember 'love'? Pitter-pat."

"Fine. Marry her." This response is news to me. Me marry Katey? Anything goes. Sounds like a nifty way of having her around. It's settled. I'll marry her.

April 6

Antony Amato owns me. He has my papers locked away in a steel drawer. "Bend over," he says and I'm quick. "Over there." Like that! I must do his will! Follow his directions. Sit up pretty when he points his finger. He has learned the secret of my universe. Without him, I am raspberry Jell-O.

Without his pointer that says do this, do that.

He is enjoying his power. Okay, we're both enjoying it. I like doing what he tells me to do. I am the original O. Are all ladies of the day and night the original O? Are all ladies such simple fucks?

And at the same time I know I'm risking everything. I say to myself every morning, I don't want to risk everything. I say to myself every morning, watch out before it's too late.

. . . I still watch Rolf sleep. Wake up fifteen minutes before he does without the alarm. I lie there, up on one elbow. I count his moles. I see new lines around his eyes. I blow air in an old bike scar. I know I am risking that right. To lie there and watch him. I know if this kid-stuff crap we're into doesn't stop, something terrible will happen, and still when the phone rings and Tony Amato says, "Now take your finger and put it up so far you can feel the inside of your belly button," I'll do it. He says, "Today you're going do me out behind the miniature golf course." I go and do.

I'm like some will-less Raggedy Ann. Anything he tells me, every day more and more outrageous. Anything he wants and more—I'd crawl through the center aisle at the PTA in my skivvies if he said so.

Why? Dear Jesus, why in hell am I doing all this?
I do it!
I think Rolf knows. I think he doesn't know.

ANTONY
April 7

Love corrupts, and absolute love corrupts absolutely.

What is this game I have been playing with Kate, this throwback to our days of pure erotica, this erogenous zone defense?

We are at the work table in my kitchen when I slip a hand between her knees, turn it like a key to open her up, and slide a fist to her privates, grind it around while making studious conversation about our book, and then, when she is dripping and twisting, pull back my hand to make an "important note."

I make her beg for it. I make her jerk and tremble for it. I play SM games out of Krafft-Ebing with her, games I thought were reserved for combatants, not lovers.

I know, way back in my corrupt brain what I am doing: I am making her need me. And I know why I am doing it: I need her.

But, oh, God, don't let me lose that beauty, that love! Please!! All I want to do is make love to her. That is all. No games.

ANTONY
April 8

Just when I thought I'd lost my sense of humor, Kate and I had a day of pure giggles.

On the way upstairs, Kate stripped to her bare bodkin, more like a boy scout late for bed check than Lily St. Cyr. When I caught up to her, I said, "You know, Kate, I always see little bits of you—a thigh, a navel, a nipple, an eyeball. How about a gander at the whole person, Katherine Edwards?"

She did a jittery pirouette and leaped into bed.

"Not so fast. It's time I took an objective look at what I'm getting into."

"It's too late," says Kate. "You've already gotten into it."

I pulled her out of bed and to the center of my bedroom. Turned on the light. Walked around her. She stood there, her hands crossed over her crotch, and made faces at me. Scrunched up her face, stuck out her tongue.

She looked lovely.

I poked at her.

"Couple of ribs showing here. Are you having any eating problems, Mrs. Edwards?"

"Yeah," Kate says, "I'm always hungry. Get into bed, will you, Tony?"

"Not so quick. Let me see those elbows. A bit chalky, what?"

"Up yours, Doctor."

"And what's this? An unbalanced bosom? Actually, it's quite common, dear. Don't worry your pretty little crazy about it."

"Don't talk to me about unbalanced, Doc. It's a well-known fact amongst all your patients that you have a mismatched set yourself—one ball off a wrecking crane and the other from a bag of marbles."

"I beg your pardon?"

"And by the way, how about taking off your frock, Doc? Even things up."

"Me, defrock myself? This is science, dearie."

I do her bidding.

"Aha," says Kate. "A defrocked gynecologist. How did it happen, you poor thing?"

" 'Twas the Pope. He said my work was keeping me off higher things."

"Like these?"

"For example."

And then she gives me inspection.

"Where's you ass?" says Kate.

"Right here. Want a closer look?"

"You call that an ass? An ass goes out, like this. That thing goes in. We call that in the literature *heinum convexus*. Very serious. But it can be cured. I'll have nurse fit you with with a corrective brace."

"Does it hurt?"

"You bet. Now let's check the nose-dick ratio. Uh-huh, uh-huh, uh-huh. Just as we suspected. You wouldn't happen to be of Eyetalian extraction would you, honey?"

"Yup. What's the troub?"

"Stand facing the wall. Yes, I was afraid of that. Nose touches first. Do you have any trouble with the normal sex act?"

"Never tried it."

And with that, we're on the floor, giggling into each other's mouths.

God, I love that woman.

KATHERINE
April 10

He's trying to get me in trouble. Told Angie. She says I'm crazy. She should talk. She's practically got the delivery boy of hers living with them. Running up three flights of stairs every time he has a can of Gerber's to drop off within six blocks of her place. At least I have the decency to do it out of the house.

Affair

"In a supermarket?"

"Not like that puny little D'Agostino's you have on Twentieth Street. I'm telling you this place must be eight blocks square."

"You did it in a supermarket?"

"Not it. I told you not it."

"Kate."

"He only used his finger."

"Oh, my God."

"Angela, he made me."

"He what?"

"You don't understand what I'm going through."

"No, I must say, I don't."

"Angie, it's wild. I love him. I tell you, he's made me stupid, a pig—a . . ."

"He stuck his finger, Katey?"

"Oh, come on, Angie what about your little schenanigans?"

"In a bedroom? You're comparing a couple of harmless sessions in between clean sheets with this . . . this . . . this . . . Kate, it's sick. You go into a supermarket, I don't care how big it is, and he sticks his hand in you? How could he stick his hand in you? Katey, you want your name spread all over the front page of that hick town newspaper?"

"Don't!"

"What do you mean, 'Don't'?"

"I'll never do it again."

ANTONY
April 10

Stop & Shop. This is public turf. I'm Kate's writing partner along for a chat while she stops and shops for the bacon. She wants me to wait for her outside, but I tail along like a helpful neighbor or son. I toss her

cereal boxes, tip my hat to fellow basket-pushers, sing
ditties about this land o' plenty. And then again I am
seized by my plight: I am an accomplice to the buying
of Rolf's groceries with Rolf's money. I am an accomplice to a crime against myself and it makes me hurt in
the balls. I have the instincts of a fascist these days, so
I move Kate playfully behind a stack of Chunky Soup
cartons waiting to be price-marked, maneuver so we
are hidden from the waist down behind this Campbell's
barricade, and there I squeeze her mound so quickly,
so knowingly, that she is struggling more against herself than against me. I work fast. I am an expert on
Katey's cunt. I know more about its ins and outs than
about anything else these days. My hand has found its
way into her panties like a divining rod. And while
Mrs. Gilicuddy passes by, nodding to us graciously as
she searches out a sumptuous soup, I am making Kate
crazy, making her come in Stop & Shop. Making her
come again and again, knowing I will pay for this and
she will pay for this, and that the end of this payment
and repayment will only come when we decide how to
do what is clear we must do. Live together!

Outside, in the parking lot, Kate does not speak. She
looks at me sadly. And I, for the first time I've known
her, look away. . . .

KATHERINE
April 11

Fidelity:
To whom do I owe it?
To whom I love?
To whom I am married?
To whom chimes my chimes?
To whom, to whom?
Very funny, except I think I know. I owe my fidelity

to whomever it is I sleep with. I am sleeping with Antony Armstrong Amato (what is his middle name?). Mrs. Antony Middlename Amato.

ITEM: Mrs. Rolf Edwards sleeps not with her husband. Her husband does not seem either to notice or mind.

ANTONY
April 13

Yes, no, yes, no, yes, no. Our days together go like yo-yos. Guilt has plagued us. Not us, her. Frustration has plagued me. One day we are indivisible lovers. The next, impossible worriers. "It's wrong." "We'll get caught." "We're being foolhardy."

I tell Kate, I explain to her, that she is missing a fundamental point. And that that is understandable because we are treading on new territory. But the point is: We have everything to gain by being together. And everything to lose by letting anything bog us down. To me, it's that simple. To me, we are the luckiest people in the world. I know this sort of thing is rare. Rarer these days than ever. To me, there's nothing relative about it. I absolutely love her. I'm sorry about Rolf, about Chris. I know it isn't simple for her, for them. I know that matters. I sympathize, empathize, try to worry with her, try to make it easier for her. But it's no use. I just want it to go away. And for Kate to stay there. I am mad. Open to anything. Like running away to Zanzibar, for example. Really, I don't care. I've got new priorities. I'm willing to give up things, too, to make this work. Trouble is, I don't have anything impressive to give up. Like wife or a job. I tell her I'll get a job by way of sacrifice. Go into banking, I tell her. And she laughs. And for a moment all is forgotten.

And then a beautiful day, without worry.

KATHERINE
April 14

Decisions are high in cholesterol. I shall give them up for Lent. I may give them up for a lot longer. Why should I? Rush into an either/or. Marry him, divorce him, face up to ambivalence, deal with realities.

TRUTH: I like my life. I like doing sexy things from 3-5, coming home to creamed asparagus and showing up for a hot round of Monopoly. The Billingses one night, the Moriaritys, another. . . . I don't want to give them up. Why should I?

FACT: I've got it pretty good, this see-saw Margery Daw, runaround I'm giving myself. I like it.

KATHERINE
April 16

"What's the matter?"

"Who said anything's—?"

"Then why aren't you sleeping?"

"I am."

"Kate?"

"Mmmm?" (Mmmm, I say to my husband, but I know what he's going to ask me and I take his hand out of habit. I know what he's going to ask me, but I have no answer.)

"Kate, what's the matter? Can't you talk to me anymore? What's eating you?"

I lie there, sucking back the tears again. All the time now, from every direction.

"Talk to me."

But I don't. I only lie there crying and know he's

123

staring at me through the darkness. I don't look at him, but don't have to. I know every pore, every crevice. We grow old, we grow old. We shall wear our trousers rolled.

"I love you," I whisper into my pillow so nobody can hear me. "I love you, I love you."

Who??????

ANTONY
April 18

In the name of the Father, the Son, and the Holy Spirit, I am a sinner. I am beyond forgiveness. I am desperate.

That quality which brought Kate and me together, that sense that we are long-lost and separated Siamese twins, is the very quality of our destruction.

Yesterday: Kate and me tooling to the Albany library for a research hit. Along the way we pass a fine old stone cathedral and we remark in unison that its image reverberates memories in our genes, so I spin the car around and park in front. We enter like brother and sister, chaste and humble, holding hands as I try the door. The inside is bare and stony like a grotto, exactly what each of us had anticipated, and now we are sure that we have been here before as our ancestors. We both dip our hands in the holy water font, genuflect, and then, each on opposite sides of the aisle, kneel as if to pray. But both of us kneel to worry. I peep across, as I did as a child, to study Katey's face, watch it contort with conflict. I am sure she would like to be out of this, that she would like to stop thinking of this as a last chance for something that transcends the rest of her life and to start thinking of it as just a last fling before she returns to her domestic compromise. She would like to kick the habit, to forget it ever happened. To be pure again. I know this. We have talked about it. I understand it. Sympathize with it. Cannot accept it. I simply cannot return to my life before Kate. I try not to be melodramatic with myself, try for what I used to call "perspective," but I am existing in a new dimension, through the looking glass. I am realer, deeper, more alive, and more myself with Kate than I have ever been. Half my life is over, and from here the first half looks trivial, at best a warm-up for this, the real half. I can only operate on this truth; the rest is foggy.

I walk to Katey and take her hand, lead her, again childlike, along the outside aisle and seeing the confessional, guide us toward it. She resists, but I am holding her strongly and smiling, now pulling us in the little cabin door, now pulling the door closed behind us.

"I love you, Kate. I want to marry you. Please."

Again, she is frightened, gives me a frightened smile and starts to leave. But I hold her and I kiss her until we both cannot breathe, until the confessional is a bomb shelter and we are refugees with only hours to live, only hours to confess our eternal love for here and hereafter.

And then I rape Katey, the woman I love. Soil her and us and the confessional and our combined memory of this church.

I am really losing control.

I don't know if I can keep this up much longer. I don't know if I will be writing this thing much longer. I just don't know what to do. I have lost my way.

KATHERINE
April 18

I am an evil woman. Last night I held my husband's hand and felt his anguish lull me to sleep. Today I

screwed my lover inside a confessional. O beautiful, O
merciless evil, I adore you, how alive you make me
feel. Forgetting anguish. Forgetting responsibility, mo-
rality, decorum, maturity, I listened to my lover give
me dirty little commands inside the confessional of my
childhood and came like the insides of my lids would
blow through the ceiling Paternoster.

"Spread your legs, my child," and I spread. "Now
lower yourself down on my upturned palm."

"Rub your breasts against my chest."

"Eat my cock."

"Squeeze," he commanded and I squeezed. Eat and
I ate. Swallow and I swallow and begged for more.

Evil isn't the word. Low-down and filthy, that's what
I am and that's what I want to be. Yes, I want a divorce. Yes, I want to bolt from hearth and home. Yes,
I want to do the devil's bidding, drink the devil's
blood.

Busty, lusty evil. It's in me raging, only I never
knew it before.

ANTONY
April 20

For comic relief, I am going crazy.

Dinner party at Preston's tonight, not unlike the one
where I met Kate. It is a reunion, and in my mind I
have been rehearsing a dramatic confrontation between
me and Rolf in front of all assembled. Instead, I find
myself in the midst of an absurd Restoration comedy.
Dining table conversation turns quickly to sex, and as
the guest swinging bachelor, I am invited to present my
firsthand sociological findings on the bedroom situation
in America today.

I tell them that there is a return to celibacy, that

people are putting the Sexy Sixties behind them so that they can get on to higher things.

Later I inform them that there is a fad in my set for making it with prepubescent girls. Somebody mentions to Kate, with a giggle, that she'd better keep an eye on Christa when I'm around. Big laugh.

Next I tell them that, contrary to popular opinion, bachelors remain that way not so much to enjoy sexual variety as to avoid the burden of a sexually demanding wife. This is my most unpopular remark of the evening, and I think it is around then that I goosed Kate under the table. And in the midst of the hubbub decided to leave. Driving off, I think I saw Kate sticking her tongue out at me from the window.

Fun, fun, fun.

I have been thinking about killing myself.

KATHERINE
April 20

We just got home from the Prestons'. Rolf's waiting for me to finish this. I can feel his hot breath through the ceiling. And his suspicions. He suspects, I know he does. He's looking at me in a new way, and not just desire. (So predictable we all are—wanting what is no longer ours.) If I were up there panting in his face, he'd suddenly have to bed down early. Something inescapable pressing like a seven-thirty appointment with the morning's *Times*. "Hurry up," he says, knowing I'm burning to write this, tonight's confession, "Hurry up," and watching my every reaction. Weighing them, as he did all night, and saying to himself, Is she or isn't she? The bastard, now, this minute as hot as Don Giovanni.

But why not when I'm the one who's hungry?

Okay, the Prestons. Awful, awful, awful. Everybody

so obvious. Everybody so business-as-usual—when it isn't. When sitting across from Tony and not being able to stare at him, to touch him, to kiss his eyes over and over, over and over, so they'll all know, so nobody else ever will sit next to him, tease him about being the perennial bachelor, fix him up. . . . If Lolly Preston says one more time she has a fantastic girl for him . . . Some fantastic girl, I know Lorraine Cherbourg, she sweats. Everything she wears, stained down to her knees.

But the way they all surrounded him. All those stodgy bored-blind, monogamous marrieds. Living on his every exploit. Pressing him against the wall for erotic details. They couldn't get enough of his titillating tales so they can all go home and relive with their eyes closed every scintillating-but-sordid tidbit. Pretending. That he's Tony. That she's the woman Tony's banging.

(Funny idea: Every man there is banging Me tonight. Spreading my legs, eating my juices. I am the woman Tony's banging. I am tonight's fantasy feature.) Yick. Who wants to go to bed with Dick Potts?

Was I blushing? Is that why I got the distinct impression, even though Tony never once looked my way, that Rolf knew? That his long-dormant wheels began finally to turn? Or, if not blush, did I stare at the floor too long? At my fingernails? Have I lived with this man for that many years that he can read my blood pressure through my Marimekko?

ANTONY
April 28

Called Kate. Rolf there again. He seems to be around more these days than when it didn't matter. She told me that we have to be careful. I told her that we have to be careful, all right, or we'd miss the biggest

opportunity of our lives. She hung up. I called back.
Rolf answered. I said, "Hi, we were cut off." When
Kate came on again, I told her I was going to fuck her
good and proper when we met again.

KATHERINE
April 29

Rolf didn't say anything. We made love. I couldn't
come. He still didn't say anything. But God knows he
must have wondered why.

ANTONY
May 1

Dear Diary,
I love Katey Edwards.
Or have I mentioned that?
We haven't done a stitch on the novel for three
weeks now.
Time for that.
And a time for love.

KATHERINE
May 3

Haven't been able to work. I sit there and my mind
just won't concentrate. It's okay. I'm about fifty pages
ahead of Tony anyway. When I work, I work fast. But
I don't like not working. It's my glue. Without this
day-in, day-out routine of mine, I'm badly unstuck. I'm

getting there. Frantic, it's called. I have to get back to
work.

Rolf's off to the city with still no word of why.
About losing the gallery. About making the rounds like
a new arrival. I feel for him. If only he'd allow himself
the sensation of feeling me feel it!

And now that he's off center stage, Chris's running a
fever (of undertermined origin, naturally). But never
mind, I know what's its origin. My kid wants a full-
time, bring-me-soda, bring-me-rock-candy, bring-me-
you, Mommy, to sit, play cards, to stay put, and never,
never to answer the phone because she knows who's
out there on the other end and she hates him. Even
though she doesn't say so or know why, my little girl
with that heavy-lidded, sick-kid look of no apparent
cause; with the movable symptoms, now you feel them,
now you're fine.

Eighteen uninterrupted gin hands. Go fish. Concentration. Backgammon. Frontgammon. A steady-ender
mommy, the two of us under her Girl Scout sleeping
bag.

The two of us reading through dinner, gossiping
about remember when I read her the Blue, Red, Green
and Yellow fairy books, brunting thighs. Loving the
scent of the other's slightly used nightgowns, never gotten out of morning to night.

A tonic they call it: Getting to know you. Time off
between times off . . . so *don't kid me, Tony whoever
you are, when you really fall in love, there's no ambivalence at all!*

Me and Chris.

Whoever you are out there, go fly a kite. Me and
Chris's busy.

Part III

ANTONY
May 9

This is the end. The triumph of evil, the destruction.
Time to pick up and go again, time to go numb again.

O Jesus, I'm scared. Been vomiting all morning.
Keep looking out the window. Is someone coming to
get me? Rolf? The police? My mother?

I'm sorry. Jesus God, I'm sorry. I've been stupid before and thoughtless and often insensitive and cavalier.
All only by way of getting by, God. Just survival. But
this one time I *wanted something*. Really wanted it,
her. And so I went crazy. I know how to do anything
but get what I want. And so I went crazy. I know how
to do anything but get what I want. Help me.

I've been fucking Kate in public places: Stop &
Shop, church, the library. Witty places, sneaky places.
But all to one purpose. To be caught. To get it out in
the open. To make something happen.

It happened. We were caught. By Chris.

By Chris, O God, the poor kid. I'm sorry.

Kate and I met last night in the parking lot next to
the supermarket. A quick rendezvous for the purpose
of—I forget. . . . ! I even forget how I got here, there.
She came, I got into her car, I pulled her down. I
raped her again.

And then I heard a scream. Chris, with a girlfriend,
looking in the window at us. At our filth. At our desperation. She screamed and ran and Katey screamed
and ran after her. I watched them run, disappear. I
waited. That is all I saw of them.

It happened. It got out of hand. Fuck all those people who say to follow your feelings, to let go, to act from the heart and guts and balls. They are wrong. Dead wrong. Love stinks. Hurts. Kills. They are right who seek the dull compromise, who avoid passion. I wish I had never met Kate. I wish I had never felt anything.

I am waiting for the end now.

I guess I will move away from here. Maybe go abroad. I don't know. I am not looking for anything. I don't want to want anything again.

I am sorry, Kate. I am sorry, Rolf, Christa, everybody. Forgive me.

Oh, Jesus God, why couldn't I have what I wanted just this once. Why?

KATHERINE
May 9

The end, the end, end. I am filth, disease, disgusting, scabrous. I hate my smell, my skin. I have sunk below skid row. There is nowhere for me. Die, die, kill myself. I am dying. I want to, have to die. The weight on my eyes in my skull is too much. Dear God, I have defiled everything . . . my life, the least. I am the spoiler. Rotten fruit staining everything else. FILTH—FILTH—FILTH, I HATE MYSELF, ripping flesh, pulling out teeth. How could I? How? How?

One more day in a series of days. The married woman has a lover. I am the married woman. I am the married woman with the lover. I eat my husband's bread, I screw someone else behind his back, never mind why. Nevermindnevermind. Just the facts. One more day in a series of defiling days. I screw my lover wherever he tells me to. However. I bend over. I kneel down. I take him, I suck him, I vibrate him. Every day stands outside of every other, and lashes them all together. It is one long, unending continuum of variations on a single theme: physical, sensual, sexual kicks, baby. Never mind who else you drag through how much mud. Who you hurt. Who you destroy. Who you ... Go on. ...

Okay, there was the bowling alley, in back. He made me, I can say. Oh, you ask? His thumb on your jugular? A knife to your solar plexus? He made you?

And after the bowling alley? On Heinrich's lawn. Out behind McDonald's. Don't forget the confessional. Can you believe you, Katherine Mary Esposito, defiled the holy Mother Church in a confessional; what more proof do you need? Just to take chances. Just to get one more thrill. One more notch. Going along. Sailing along. Fun and games, come and come again. Till now when you have destroyed everything. Everything. Everything. What's wrong with you? Is nothing real in your life anymore? Real. With substance and values. Perspective, you bitch. Did the worst never occur to you?

"Mommy?" she said.

"Mommy???" and I looked up to find the small, frightened face of my little Christa staring in the window of the car with her ice cream dripping down the side of her hand into her sleeve. All she could say was "Mommy," over and over again, but it was enough. It's a sound I'll have to live with forever. Cutting off my blood between my black soul and my guts.

KATHERINE
May 10

No sound. I have seashells down my ears. The childhood tide coming in on me, wave after wave of no sound. Nausea, without nausea. Not even tears. Finished. Don't even want to die. Want nothing.

ANTONY
May 10

What am I going to do? Please, somebody help me. What should I do? Please.
I wish Willie were here.
I don't know what to do.

KATHERINE
May 10

In three weeks Chris's out of school. I am afraid.
I read my Diary which said, "Chris watches me with the piercing-crow look, her eyes pinioned to my liver." (She was two.) My fingers are cold. I am running an untemperature.

KATHERINE
May 11

No pulse. Rolf Edwards is singing upstairs. The Museum Either With or Without Walls has commissioned a mural, is putting him in its catalog, refers to him as a hard-edger's hard-edger. They are right. He wants to fuck.

It's four-something in the morning and in the dark of Chris's room her eyes shine up at me like pea-coat buttons. "Please, Chris, say something; there's so much about tomorrow you can't possibly understand."

Please, Chris, please, Chris, please, Chris. . . .

I am freezing. It's May and I'm wearing sheepskin boots and each toe stands at cold attention trying to hold me up. My eyes throb. I have rigor mortis of my hope. *And upstairs my stupid husband has fucking on his mind.* What's the matter with me, he wants to know? Either I crawl the walls like Maggie the cat, or go encephalitic on him??????

I live only with Sartre's permission. Frozen stiff. I'm so cold.

I know I have to tell Rolf.

I know I have to.

I know I have to, I have to get the weight off Chris's shoulders. I have to. I have to.

Except what if it all explodes?

I'm in the dream where you run and run and get noplace. I holler out, I make my clean breast, I come clean just as loud as I can.

Can't stand it, it's killing her. Why can't I tell him? Why am I suddenly so afraid if he finds out I'll have taken Chris over the Rubicon with me and that neither of us'll ever be able to cross back over again? Isn't that what I wanted?

ANTONY
May 12

I don't know what to do. I can't get out of bed. I
called Ted today. Hung up when his wife answered.

I'm running out of food.

KATHERINE
May 13

I listen while everybody else sleeps. The hairs on my
arms listen. I dare not relax my vigilance. . . . For
when she tells him who I really am. Who he's been living with all these years. The listening hairs on my arms
get so cold they break off like peanut brittle.

"What do you want for breakfast?" I ask her, the
cords on the side of my neck as yellow as pencils, but
she won't answer me or swallow anything.

Rolf sort of notices something funny, cause he says,
"What's the matter with her?" Only he doesn't wait for
an answer. Just as well; am I supposed to say she holds
the key to all our tomorrows in her pinafore? That I'm
in terror she'll tattle. Rip us apart, memory from good
times, tomorrow from the fatal yesterday.

"Who knows?" I shrug, trying to touch her before
she runs off to the sixth grade. With no success.

"Nope, she doesn't look right," he says later, but
again, before I have to agree with him, he does Hou-
dini for me.

"By the way," he says, "I'm not with Edmond anymore, but don't sweat," snapping his fingers, "Eisley
snapped me up like that!"

"Eisley?" I say, impressed, and my quick-change

138

husband has made his quick change. The silent, brooding crisis has been vacuumed up from under the rug and he's once more on top of things. "What about you and me, we go upstairs and knock off a slow one?"

Then, barely back to Chris again, "Sure, something's eating her," but for all he knows it's the Friday afternoon geography test, ones-on-time-follow contest tournament. ... What does he know?

Nothing, I think to myself. . . . Please, Chris, give me another chance? Mothers are also people, Chris. Other connections? A small, barely perceptible existence outside the four walls of your understandings?????

"La donn' é mobile," my husband sings, grabbing for me. . . . "Let's you and I go climb Lookout Point," and then fuck on the top, I suppose? Now that everything hangs by a silk thread from Chris's belly button to the sling attached to my sanity?

Disequilibrium: The word for the hour. And how come the astronauts in *Life* magazine know how to eat eye of the round and play bridge?

Now? Lookout Point? You had to wait till now? Lookout Point has been there all year, dammit.

ANTONY
May 13

First, I have to find out if Kate is all right. Just find out. Not speak to her. Not yet. I have to find out if she's all right first.

That's what I have to do first. I cannot think about what to do until after that.

It wasn't dark until after nine tonight. I dressed in black and blue, turtleneck, jeans, and Willie's dancing shoes.

I am in a movie. The only way I can move is by being in a movie. It is a French movie, I think. *La Nuit Folle.*

I drive out of town the long way, over the thruway and then backtrack through Carson's dairylands. I try listening to the radio. I pick up Leon Lewis taking a call from Queens. A man in a phone booth wants to know if Jesus could have been black. Leon says it is unlikely. The man says Jesus had soul and that's why he asks. Leon says we all have soul, black and white alike. Off with the radio.

As I pass de Fries' chinchilla ranch, I find myself mumbling in Italian. *Per favore. Per favore. Non domando questo favore solamente per me. E per mia Katrina—solamente per Katrina.* The voice of the child in my guts. It speaks Italian.

And then I sing. "Chattanooga Choo Choo." "Peg o' My Heart." "Wanted." Unconsciously, I am soon doing my Perry Como imitation. The one that used to leave Franco in convulsions. For the background of "Wanted," I sing "Pope-pope-pope-pius" instead of "Pa-pa-pa-paya." I never did that one for Kate. Since Franco, she's the only one who would have laughed.

A man could do Perry Como imitations on the way to a funeral. Anna Karenina was thinking about lip rouge when the train split her skull. Our last thoughts are trivial because our lives are trivial. What's the question, Alice B.?

And then, nothing. Gliding through the night, past

trees and hedges, an occasional house with lights burning downstairs. (All houses passed on a dark nights are happy ones overflowing with family feeling.)

And then Cliff Road. I pull over onto the shoulder and click off the ignition, the lights. I step out, quietly close the door behind me, and I am in the movie again.

Long shot as Mad Tony steals through the pine grove to the high grass. Close-up as he peers into the distance, trying to find his bearings. Pan as he races through the high grass, his ankles stung by nettles. Long shot, Mad Tony's P.O.V. as he peers past the oaks to the rear of the house Edwards.

Katey's house. What am I doing here? What in the name of God am I doing here? There are lights on downstairs ("All happy families are happy in the same way") and moving shadows. There's life in there, sure as shooting. I creep closer. Some of the light is blue. TV light. They are watching television!!! Katey has obviously committed suicide and the family is having a television wake. The mourners are watching "Medical Center" for catharsis. Closer.

And I see her! My Katey! My love! Jesus God, there she is in the kitchen window. Hello, Kate! Hello, my love! Run away with me, Kate! She is doing something with her hands. Slitting her wrists, perhaps?

No, peeling carrots!

I raced back to the car, jumped in, and pulled out onto the road. Faster, faster. Past the lake. Laughing, nay, giggling. It's a farce. The movie, my life, Katey and me. It's a goddamned farce.

Laughing until the tears run down my face.

Crying until the tears run down my face.

KATHERINE
May 14

Chris's definitely watching me. (My left leg is so cold I can hardly stand.)

If I go to the john I can feel her walk by. If I'm cooking. She's always on her way somewhere. Just passing through. She doesn't leave me alone for a moment. Afraid of what I'll do next? Then why don't I save her? Why can't I save her?

KATHERINE
May 15

I don't answer the phone. I know it's him and don't know what to say.

Dreamed about Vic Straccusi and high school. How I stopped seeing him because of his nails. From one morning to the next. The love of my life and then, Bingo. No more. Suddenly, I couldn't stand seeing those nails bitten beyond the quick. Irrational, the way I cut off Vic Straccusi. And there is no parallel. I do not love Tony Amato. Sublimation is a strong somethingorother.

I explained everything to Chris. Through the closed door of her room. She still won't say anything. I don't blame her. The League of Decency would have banned me too.

ANTONY
May 15

This is ridiculous (I decided at breakfast), I'm going to call her. The fact is, nothing really happened at all. Chris came home and Katey asked her what the problem was. "After all all we were doing in the car was looking for some papers that got lost under the seat. What upset you, sweetie? Did you think he was hurting me? That skinny little fellow? He couldn't hurt a flea. Now what shall we make for dinner for Daddy-wad-dums, huh, sweetie?"

And that was that.

She's just waiting for me to call.

It was just a little scare, a warning. We really have to be more careful. I'll promise her no more public places. I'll promise her any goddamn thing she wants, for that matter.

But I can't stand this silence anymore!

Morning: No answer.

Noon: Busy signal.

Afternoon: Chris answers, I hang up.

That was my day, Diary. The day of a fully grown (fully grown? How about rapidly decaying?) man. The same man who, as a student of post-Kantian idealism at Harvard, promised himself to lead a unique life.

KATHERINE
May 16

Walked back and forth in front of St. Anthony's just so I could cross myself.

I am afraid. Dear Jesus, I am afraid of my own

daughter. She holds the power of my To Be or Not to Be in her hands and I don't know how to rescue her. I cannot just say the magic words to Rolf. I cannot and must. She is also on my hook.

Do you know where your daughter is this moment?

KATHERINE
May 17

Like a slut, like slut's spawn? Whore, little whore? Not one word in more than a week, dressing up like June Allyson trying to be Jane Withers trying to be Jayne Mansfield. Yesterday I watched her stop in front of the kitchen window and change her clumpy boys' sneakers for a pair of black suede "pumps" that I picked up at the Junior League shop for a fifties bengaline I never wore either.

And lipstick.

Rolf hasn't seen her. She takes it off again before she comes home. But she knows I'm watching. And she knows there isn't a damn thing I can do about it.

And then she stares at me and spreads out her nostrils. She won't let me read to her, talk to her, be with her, tell her, beg her . . . nothing. There is no charity in my daughter. She's got me in a tiger cage and has every intention of keeping me there. While I beg her with my eyes, don't, Christa. . . . Don't say anything we'll both be sorry for.

ANTONY
May 18

Kate answered. Before I could say a word, she said, "I can't talk now" and hung up.

How did she know who it was?

Or did she?

She has a new lover. It was all a setup. Chris's in on it. Chris has a lover, too. They're in cahoots.

Oh, shit, what is going on? Day after day I do nothing. What about the book, Kate? Huh? Remember the book? Remember "what a nifty way to work"? Remember fun?

I am stuck.

KATHERINE
May 18

Funny, in a strange way Rolf and I have sort of picked up our old ways without a word. Some days we make love. Some days we don't. He lets his ass rub mine in bed without that vein of resistance up to his earlobes. He picks conversations instead of fights. He never refers to me as a nymphomaniac.

He thinks Chris's not talking to me is average crap. That's the way they are, he says. She'll get over it.

It's been ten days to the day. To what day? he'd say. He doesn't know. Chris doesn't seem to want to tell him. I don't know. Can something like this just blow over?

ANTONY
May 19

I am paralyzed.
I write letters. I tear up letters. I cancel myself out.
I am dead.

KATHERINE
May 19

The illusion of normal, only Chris's steel-belted eyes
screwed to our secret knowledge. Tony doesn't call. I
don't know anybody named Tony.

KATHERINE
May 22

Time refuses to heal all wounds. Chris, I'm afraid, is
bent on paying too dearly. Refuses intervention. Yesterday, I swear, she was wearing an uplift. No longer
bothers to remove the eye shadow before coming
home.

ANTONY
May 25

This evening I took out the atlas. That, for me, is al-
ways a sign of life. I will move my body to new soil.
I love her. I still love her so much.
I look at relief maps . . . the steppes of Central
Asia, pink with vertigo. The boulders of Holland, blue
with aquaphobia.
I could never leave her. Never.
Antarctica looks appealing. So does Tierra del
Fuego. San Salvador. Rio.
Never.

May 26

Enough! Neither of us can or should take anymore. Instead of driving her directly home after school, we head for the scene of my crime. Direct confrontation. While I try to crack her Lucite shell for the millionth time.

"Chris," I start, watching the road, "you've got to understand. I love you Christa. Don't forget the twelve years of oatmeal I made with raisins. You can't just drop a mother over four grisly minutes in a supermarket parking lot; who knows what uses you may still have for me, Chris?

"Chris?"

A child of the snapping turtle. Whose head would have to be chopped off before she'd let go. Of her mad. Her frenzy. Her locked-in confusion. After all . . . I was her mother. Mother's are supposed to be through with "all that." They're supposed to sink quietly into first their assigned roles and then their graves. No regrets. No bothersome stinks. There is no room for variation, Mother. None. . . . So from now on Chris's going to be too old for a mother. Her mother will be as dead as my own. . . .

"No!" I begged her. "Look at me, Chris. . . . Why are you turning everything on yourself?. I won't let you." I told her. I tried burning my worry, my cares, my eyes, my wants for her into her. Into her skin. Into her suffering little soul, only all I got was the rigid turn of her shoulder as it slid still farther onto the far end of the seat we shared.

Sounds of an incoming tide against my eardrum. Of the car shuddering as I turned first left into the lot and then as I turned off the key. Sounds of us sitting.

Silently. The hollow hit of my forehead against the steering wheel.

"You need me, baby. . . . When you try to figure this kind of thing out by yourself, all you get is the wrong answer. . . ."

No answer.

"Chris," I begged. "Chris . . ." crying, me. Christa long since gone to chip-proof plastic.

"Listen to me, Christa. If you'll give me only one small chance to make it up . . . to . . ." To nothing. To hell and back. To the right! FACE!!

Zero. Even though, believe me, I knew better; Didn't I know it could happen to almost anybody? What about all the other nice, middle-aged mothers we all knew in common? Chris, what are you going to say when *you* get there? Old age—this way—What if you can't hack it the way it says in *Little Women* either?

"I'm sorry," I said. "Oh, God, Chris, if you only knew how much I wish I could shove the whole thing back onto the drawing board and . . ." And then, sitting there pounding my mind against that perfectly formed sound-proofing of hers, I gave up. I saw the bulb at the end of the tunnel turn from faint to out. I knew it was no use. I knew it and got out.

Of the car.

For what exact reason I didn't know. To find in the lines painted on the vast vale of concrete the way into my daughter? To beat my breast out under the sky? Holy Mother help me, now and at the hour of my death. . . . And then for some eerie feeling I turned back toward the car and watched my sweet little child slide across the seat till she'd positioned herself behind the steering wheel.

"What for, Christa? You can't drive," I said, as she first locked the door and then turned the key, started the engine and jerkily backed up the Saab between two parked cars as easy as pie.

"But you can't, Chris," I said, watching her. What?

What can't she? She was. Or maybe you can't do this emotionally, only that was happening, too, right in front of my eyes. She was every which way driving off, leaving me.

And then I thought, How was it I'd gotten out? No, I hadn't remembered wanting out. "Christa!" Suddenly screaming. Suddenly coming to and running after her. "Christa, be careful. Christa!" as she carefully passed rows C, D, E, and F, meticulously avoiding a Chevy pickup on its way in, and then headed right straight for the streetlight embedded in the island just before the Entrance and Exit signs.

I think I called her name again. Or maybe I didn't, as the light bulb tinkled into shards as it hit the hood. But I do remember saying quite clearly that at that speed, don't worry, nothing could have happened to her. Nothing as simple as an injury. And she'd already been in shock a long time and seemed to be used to it.

Shock. That's what it was. Of identifiable source. I felt more like my own mother every minute. Holding my little baby. Caressing her limp and peaceful form. Shock was a blessing. I even tried to catch some for myself. To fuzz the edges off the rest of what now had to finally come, finally. Once the hospital assured me I was right; nothing as simple as an injury had happened.

Out of shock, she wouldn't let me touch her or even stay in the room. If there was a battle of wills in progress, Chris won. I left and everybody started picking up their losses.

Walked down ramp from Emergency. Called Rolf.

Called a cab. If the cab cost six dollars. Was I in shock? Chris, room, no money?

Rolf got home at 5:45.

"What's the matter with you?" he said. "Where's the car?"

I said, "Can we go for a ride in yours?"

"Chris?"

"I'll tell you everything in the car, please," I said. "It'll be nice" (maybe the last few nice moments). "It's O.K.," I said. O for Over; K: Katherine, Kayoed, Kahflochie. . . . "Let's just go," that's all I knew. In the car his hands'll be occupied. He'll have to watch the road. In the car, the car . . . where somehow for the while we'd all be safe, *as if nothing had happened.*

Eyes closed, head turned out the window, Katherine Edwards says, "I've been having an affair with Tony Amato; don't be mad." As she is not looking directly at him, she does not see him either flinch or not.

"Anyway, it's over."

All she knows for sure is that the car continues to drive. Quite a time goes by. Rolf says nothing. Ultimately, Katherine says, "Rolf?"

He responds by asking me—her, "That's what you had to tell me?"

She shakes her head.

"Can we go home now?"

"Are you mad at me?"

And again there is no answer. Again she says, "Rolf?"

The silence is quite noticeable.

"Anyway, it was awful," Rolf misunderstands.

"What? Screwing Tony Amato?"

"No," she says, very, very low. "About Chris."

Now his reaction is immediate. "What's Chris got to do with it?" The time for Katherine to soft-shoe her way out has sifted out the hole that has been in the bottom all along.

"Oh, God," she says, with horrible anguish. "Rolf, she saw us."

The car lurches.

"She what?"

Kate's body is thrown forward, and for the first time in their marriage, Rolf does not put a protective arm out to catch her.

"What do you mean she saw you?"

"There is no way to tell you so you'll understand."

"A little late for the fine shading, don't you think?"

"I told you it was horrible."

"Goddamn it, Kate."

And again Katherine looks out the window. She says, without really moving her lips, "We were in the Stop and Shop parking lot."

"The . . . ?"

"I told you, you wouldn't understand."

"You were screwing in a public parking lot? Chris saw her mother screwing in a parking lot? Is that what you're telling me?"

(The voice so laden with horror Katherine saw how it looked from the point of view of the sane.)

"Oh, my God," she said. The idiot speaks. "Oh, my God, Rolf. No, it didn't happen. We'll go away. We'll . . ."

"Shut your sewer, you bitch. Where is she?"

"I'm afraid." (Katherine heard herself say I'm afraid, because she was.)

"Bullshit, you're afraid . . . you and that . . . I'll break his little wop cock for him. . . . *I asked you where is she?????*" and he jammed the brakes so furiously, he streaked the highway with a black scar.

"No," she moaned, "if I tell you, the hospital, you'll . . ."

"Hospital?"

"It isn't. No, Rolf, it's not . . . she's not . . . She's all right, Rolf, believe me. . . ."

"Chris's at the hospital?"

"Rolf?"

He was looking at me and hearing what I'd been saying.

I came to.

"Rolf, Chris's all right. Physically, I mean. They only took her to . . ."

"Get out," he said. He opened the door and couldn't look at me anymore.

"Don't leave me here," I nattered. Nattered is the exact word. "I didn't mean it," did I have the nerve to say "no, really, what you could call hospital requirements, Rolf . . ."

I thought again of Count Leo Tolstoy and the truth of a clean suicide! Two seconds and it's over. A smear of red next to the black scar up the center of the highway. The Red and the Black. Anna Karenina and Julien Sorel.

My God, how I loathed myself. No ambivalence at all.

A car came from around the curve and I stood up in preparation for the impact. I closed my eyes. And then I moved out of range, too chicken even to imagine myself as the sackful of dog do the guy'd think he'd hit.

And then I did another loathsome thing.

I sat by the side of the highway saying Chris's name over and over, exactly as I'd done as a child when I couldn't sleep. When I'd call out the name of Sister Mary Agnes who used to teach the The Holy Apostles and didn't anymore, or sometimes Melanie Wilkes. "Melanie . . . Melanie," I used to call into the night *because it made me feel better*.

The same way I sat there in the wind and called for my daughter.

DATELESS IN GAZA

The quality of fear is subzero worthlessness. Covered with spit.

I now knew who I was. While Christa needed me.

Seeing myself sitting there feeling sorry for Katherine. Poor Katherine, her mommy is dead. Where is Katherine's mommy?

"Christa," she called, but wasn't it really, "Mama"?

Oh, baby, Christa, if I am all you have to turn to: run! Wherever you fetch yourself up, you'll be better off.

A mother who can't even commit suicide.

Who longs for her own mother when you need her.

Who has been down so far it looks like down to her.

It must have been a very long time that I sat there thinking about throwing myself under the passing cars, but not actually doing it. Thinking of my mother. Thinking of when Chrissy used to love to rub her skin against mine.

A very long time between one loathsome act and the next.

The next being picking myself up and going, instead of to my just punishment . . . back to my lover's.

I went to my lover's.

When my child lay in the hospital, where did I go? I went to my lover's.

"I'll never leave you again," my lover said, and his words hung around my neck like a day-old doughnut.

To be frigid is to watch another person make a fool of himself.

I am coming down off a six-month high.

Really down.

My lover touches me and I feel my mother's dead clammy hands.

To be frigid is sobering.

To be frigid is a relief.

At least, Dear Diary, when I went to my lover's I had the bottom-line decency at least to be frigid.

ANTONY
May 26

I can barely write tonight. I have been sick. There is vomit streaked on the back-door window of my car which I spat out while driving home, afraid if I stopped, I'd stop for good.

I saw Katey. For the first time in how long? Two, three weeks? I've lost count.

She called. "I'm coming," she said, that's all. "I'm coming," her voice sharp and brittle, like cracked ice. And I stood there by the kitchen phone, heard the click, the buzz, the dial tone. Who? Who's coming? Why?

And then she came.

Dear God, something has happened to Kate! Some disease. Some curse. She is evaporating. She has turned to liquid and now is evaporating.

"Kate! Dear Kate!" I held her, but where is she? I kiss her hair, but it is cobwebs on my tongue. I look in her eyes and see only my reflection. She is here in my kitchen at last! But she is missing. A lost person.

"What is it, Kate? What's happened?"

She shrugs.

"Kate, what's wrong? I'll call a doctor."

She shakes her head.

"Sit down. I'll make tea. Or a drink? Do you want a drink?"

She stands by the kitchen door, looking toward the stairs. There is no weight to her and no color. Have I been alone for so long? Have I dreamed and rehearsed this meeting so often that now, in reality, it can only have marginal existence?

"Kate, it's me, Tony. I've missed you incredibly. I've been worried, sick, crazy. Kate, Kate. I love you so much."

"Yes," Kate says. "Love. Make love to me."

And we walk up the stairs, slowly, not touching. Like prisoners to our cell.

"Hold me, Kate. Please, hold me, touch me, talk to me."

"I have to get undressed," she says.

She is wearing the same denim skirt and yellow

cardigan that I have seen on her and on my bedroom chair (and floor) a hundred times. But today, they are sackcloth, potato bags she is twisting out of. And, when she flops on my bed, I can barely see her. My unchanged sheets have turned to the color of wax paper, and Kate has changed to the color of my sheets.

We made love. Nay, I made love. Nay, I pantomimed lovemaking, pantomimed kisses and licks, shifts and thrusts. A solo performance.

Was she even watching?

"Kate, please. Please, God, what has happened?"

"Nothing."

"Nothing? Nothing? Is Chris all right? Is Rolf—"?

"Shut up. Shut up, Tony." This said quietly, almost in a whisper. Then, "I have to go. Will you drive me?"

I drove her (she had come by cab) over the same back roads I took last week to watch her peeling carrots. No words. No signs. Not a touch, a thought, a vibration.

At Route 9A, she said, "Stop. I'll walk from here."

"Walk? Where? You're miles from—"

"Let me out. Now."

"Kate. Please don't do this to me. Talk to me. Anything. Is it over? Are you sick? Talk to me. Tell me. I won't do anything, but—"

And the door slams shut. I follow her for a while.

"Go, Tony. Leave me. I have to be alone."

And, as I turn the car and drive off, I feel the sickness beginning in my gut that spattered out the window and back against my face. I understand nothing. I feel nothing.

I wish she had never come. Ever. She is death.

KATHERINE
May ?
The hospital

Same day? Another day? Night? Same? I don't remember. I don't deserve such information.

Liar: Hospital, Later: After I didn't kill myself. After I went and did the same thing all over again even after all my phony protestations. *Even after she still lay here on her back; what is the matter with me??????????*

The hospital: A cream and brown place that is dirty, all over. With the Irish nurses from my appendix in the same pink and white smiles. And a Fire Door, with a crucifix over it, that's really just swinging glass that would burn like crazy. Where Catholics come because it smells like home.

I walk up three flights because I don't deserve the convenience of the elevator.

I go into my child's room and disturb the symmetry. I bring in the cold. (*The smell of another man's body touching mine,* even though it didn't work. See, Rolf, it didn't work. . . . Doesn't that prove something? I bring in my body. It is a week-old salmon with blue gills that reek of old age.)

There is a film of unseeing gray across my husband's eyes. He is my husband. His eyes glisten tearlessly. He does not flinch when I crawl in on my belly to stare at my little girl who will not stare back at me. I force myself not to sing to her. She doesn't need the sound of my phony songs down her sleep.

Nobody looks up when I come in, so I am not there.

The light down the hall over the nurses' station is faint in the distance. There's always a 40-watt darkness in the room. I see Rolf's eyes concentrating on the line of stitching around his toes. I can see my whole life running in front of my pain like a pack of lemmings on LSD.

Black is the color of my true love's hair.

Chris's is blond. Rolf's is blond. Mine is red. Blood red. I am a Fellini gargoyle on the end of a cathedral spire, peering down into my own entrails, through the stained-glass window of my bad deeds.

I AM DYING. Sitting up, singing to my drugged daughter and my husband, there, who can't look at me. I will walk through the shadow of the kingdom of death, on nettles and prickles and gooseberry patches. . . . Drowning in peroxide to bleach my false colors. . . . I am already dead. I will run down the grayed-over, cream-colored hospital hallway to steal the deadly nightshade phial in the glassed-in cabinet, locked and shackled . . . suddenly down on my knees whimpering at the bottom of her bed.

"Stop it," he said. "This is no time for upstaging," and then the feel of his hand almost on the fringe of my head, almost petting the fuzz of my hair, almost able to touch, almost.

"She'll need you. Goddammit—shape up."

But when I went to hold onto his legs, and press my penance so tightly about him he couldn't walk away from it, he did.

Shaking his head.

"More bullshit. You're going to just have to cope."

"Okay," I said, "go home. One of us has to get up in the morning." I didn't look up to see him not look down at me. Just listened to the hush of crepe soles pause and then go through the door and down the still hospital hall, over my shivering.

My sleeping daughter has warts on her thumbs, spunkwater, spunkwater. She has tiny moons and smaller fingers. And her whole life is ahead of her. I cannot let her settle for "and then they'll be sorry," fantasies.

I will not allow two lousy minutes in some parking lot to take that kind of hold on her life.

I will not allow it.

I move my chair closer to the window where, by the streetlamp I write:

Chris shall have her head shrunk.
I shall have my head shrunk.
He shall have his head shrunk.

Signs and symbols in Christian Art.
When was the last time Christa did a handstand against the icebox?
Tony Amato is an old boyfriend.
The reason you do not jump in front of cars is you do not want to jump in front of cars.
You lost your skate keys and lived through it.
Sex is sublimated happiness.

ANTONY
May 27

Found out today (Lolly Preston) that Chris Edwards is in the hospital. Had an accident trying to drive her mother's car. Nothing serious. "But don't call," Lolly says. "Rolf and Kate are terribly upset and aren't seeing people just now."

So that is it. Ugliness upon ugliness. We must suffer more. We must pay and pay and pay until we are empty. And even then not be forgiven.

I will wait and wait until I am empty.

And I will erase yesterday from my memory forever.

June 4

I have lost eight pounds. Over how long, I don't know.

I called Didi, who called a friend who worked with a doctor who works with kids. He said he'll see Chris—somehow her going will have to be separate from ours. Our shrink, her shrink—just to make one day to the next? Rolf doesn't want to, but will. And he's still here.

"Cope," he says. . . . Okay, I'm coping.

Chris comes home today and we'll see. I'm finished begging her. Here I am, I didn't kill anybody. If she wants me to make her oatmeal with raisins, I'l make it. If she wants French toast, all she has to do is ask.

Or go somewhere else with Rolf? We'll see. So far he's here. I sound like an ad for Dale Carnegie. Before or After? I don't know that either.

Angie and Sam are getting a divorce. I called Dr. B. for the courage to go to this marriage genius with Rolf. Dorcas will be separated a year. Marvie still doesn't talk to her. Never liked Dr. B. No wonder I'm crazy.

Spent the morning on the john thinking about Tony, why I couldn't, and the myth that sex is what Capuchins are sublimating by not talking. And it is a myth. I've been there. . . . I swear it's the other way around. It's everything else we're all trying to find between the sheets.

"I love you," I can say to any passing stranger, but if Rolf leaves me, my inside will hollow out. "I love you"; can I say that to Rolf? I will never make a sharpshooter, always watching too many angles at once.

A stranger can't *really* hurt. He can only pass on.

To be vulnerable is to be abandoned. Old lessons die hard. Like mothers.

If Rolf leaves me I will donate my body to Columbia Presbyterian.

KATHERINE
May 28—night

Open all the windows, let the night humors come in.

I told my husband if I hadn't gone out and done what I'd done, I'd have envied my daughter's growing up and away. Didn't he understand?

He didn't say.

But he didn't leave either. So far he's still here.

ANTONY
June 5

I, who never quite got the hang of writing television soaps, have discovered that my real talent is for living them.

And how I long for a commercial interruption.

I should be falling apart. But I am laughing tonight. Those are my only two remaining activities: falling apart and laughing.

This evening after dinner (the fifth in this week's series of Kraft delicacies), I continued going through my papers. I am putting things in order these days. It gives me a sense of continuity. It reminds me there was life Before Kate (BK). Old story ideas. Unfinished pilot plans. Unmailed letters. Tax returns. Lists: books to read, places to go, people to call. Rules for living: up early, no smoking, exercise, no TV. I was filing these when I heard a car pull in the driveway.

Kate! Oh, God, Kate! Back at last, back to normal, back to—

But no, it is not Kate. Close, but not Kate. It is Rolf!

Rolf Edwards, the husband. The winner.

"May I come in?"

"Yes, sure. Want something to drink?"

"So here's where it all happened, eh, Amato?"

"How's that, Rolf?"

"I said, 'Here's where it all happened.' You know what I'm talking about."

"The book?"

"Cut the crap, Amato. I know about you, about you and Kate."

(My laughter, tonight, begins with the way I hear Rolf speak. His lines, the very cadences of his speech, are clearly not his; they are imitations drawn from films, novels—TV! And, after all, why not? Where else do we learn how to handle such situations as this? Where else do we witness the Husband and the Lover face to face except on the tube?)

"Oh . . . I see."

Remember when you ached for this moment, Tony? When you thought the only way for you and Kate to make it would be for this precise denouement to come about? And now, what do you have to say? What can you say about a thirty-five-year-old woman who has turned everybody's life upside down?

Rolf: It was sex, wasn't it?

Me: Amongst other things.

Rolf: What other things?

Me: Love. Love was one of the other things.

Rolf: You're full of shit.

Me: That, too. That's one of the other things.

And Rolf laughs, an interior sort of hiccough chortle. "Jesus Christ, you sound just like her. 'Love,' 'shit,' all in the same breath. It's all the same to you, isn't it?"

Me: No, it's not. Believe it or not, my heart is broken, Rolf.

And then silence. Rolf paces around my kitchen, looking at things, poking at things. The detective looking for clues. The critic gauging my aesthetic. Then into the living room which is overwhelmed by precarious stacks of papers and folders, maps and books. I suppress the urge to say, "If I had known you were coming, I'd have straightened up a bit." My mother, sizing up the situation, would have thought me rude not to at least make some excuse for the mess.

And then upstairs where he checks out the bathroom, Willie's guest room, my bedroom.

"So, here's where you fucked her, eh?"

No comment.

"Or is it where you 'made love'?"

"Yes."

"You made love here, but you fucked her in parking lots, right?"

This man is easily one-and-a-half times my weight and could, with a well-placed chop or two, make me dead. Or he could scream. Or he could cry. Instead, he turns and looks at me, a soft-eyed man, and says, "Jesus Christ, you even look like her," and walks down the stairs. I follow him to the door where he turns again and says, "I hate your fucking guts" (as if it were something he had almost forgotten to tell me.)

How easily I could think of him as a brother.

How sure I am that he is not.

KATHERINE
June 6—morning

"How come?" he wanted to know. "Have I ever denied you anything?"

He asked me in the purest innocence.

And the gall rose to my surface and threatened to choke the two of us with the same swell.

A week left to school. Chris is very weak, and suddenly looks very tiny. She doesn't seem to care there's only a week left to school. But she doesn't want to go either. She wants to lie in her room and read Laura Ingalls Wilder. *The Long Winter.*

It's both the best and worst selection she might have made.

We've come through! D. H. Lawrence. The same story.

I can't stand it. She's too tiny for all of this.

KATHERINE
June 7

Chris wanted macaroni and butter. No sauce. She only ate half of that.

Rolf bought her a cowboy hat and a paper bag filled with penny candy. Mostly fish. They'll share.

I want to watch "All in the Family" with them but don't know how.

Rolf sits up way past Johnny Carson. I never feel him slip in or out of bed. Maybe he doesn't.

My temperature is 97.

It's June already and I'm still sleeping in sheepskin slippers.

KATHERINE
June 8

"Try it," I told Chris who doesn't want to talk to this psychiatrist. "You're the one who's screwed up,"

she says, and where do I come off arguing with her?
She is at least talking.

"You'll feel better," I say weakly, and am afraid to
say, "Please," but she's too debilitated to put up much
resistance. She lets Rolf take her, but before leaving,
she says it again.

"You're the one who's screwed up," and stares right
through the leftover parts of me which have always
been on her side.

"It's all right," I say, "I'll be here when you get
back," and so somehow I know she knows that until
Rubberman flies through the window, that and the Red
Cross is all there is.

They left, and then, I have to admit it, I heard myself humming, *Come to me, quietly, do not do me injury, Gently, Johnny, my Gigolo.*

The same inflection, the same phrasing, the same
sound of Richard Dyer Bennett from tenth grade.

I am either screwed up, like Chris says, or somehow
primitive in my insistence upon survival. Not sure
which. Will ask new head-fixer Rolf and I see Wednesday, 4:00.

KATHERINE
June 10

All psychiatrists save the prints from their first
apartment to hang in their waiting rooms. The prints
divide into two camps. The lone cowboy who stands
against the skies-that-are-not-cloudy-all-day and the
more cultured, Kandinsky for the millions, variety.

Dr. Schwartz is your cultured, art-loving head-fixer.
Who is also too young and too tall. When a doctor is
that tall and that young, confidence is lost. *Do not take
my laughing on the outside* as an accurate description
of my state of mind. I am merely hysterical since my

husband and I come to Dr. Schwartz, A. for the sake of our child and B. to save our marriage. Two hysteria-provoking reasons.

I have dressed meticulously. Even my nails are pared. I want to make a good impression even though this boy is too young to save either our marriage or our child.

SESSION:

Hello. My name is.

Then the awkward silence.

Then Rolf, who wants to forget it all. Who has A wife who hadn't played by the rules. Who had been LET DOWN.

I let Rolf talk. I know he needs to GET IT OUT. I have come here to be gotten back in line. No, seriously, I have come because I know I need to come. I close my eyes and listen to Rolf.

Rolf says his resentment will pass. He'll get over it. He says the trouble with American women is they lack realistic goals. They share romantic pipe dreams with their girlfriends over the telephone. For hours. What do they think? he says. That life is easy? Do they think all life is is sitting on their cans on the telephone? It would be the best thing in the world if this liberation jazz really did take hold, he says. It would give them a taste of the hard knocks out there in the real world. Though he doesn't bear me any resentment. Actually I'm only a victim. Of the media. It isn't my fault. Overstimulation, that's what it is. I've always needed a monkey on a string. Every minute a new song and dance. It isn't really my fault.

I am more to be pitied than censured.

There's really nothing he has to say.

So he doesn't say anything.

I open my eyes.

See the funny lady? Stuff her with a 107 IQ. Add silicone. Attach to telephone.

Even Rolf has to laugh.

He does, shaking his head, and finally letting it fall (his head) into his hands.

"I don't know," he says in a low voice. "Maybe I'm not the easiest guy to get along with either."

"Sure you are, honey," I say. I whimper and take his hand. *Am I looking for points?* I go back to my chair and feel like a cheat.

"Well, Mrs. Edwards? What do you have to say?" I look up at him and know he had a hard time with his Ph.D. bedside manner requirement. I, too, have nothing to say for myself besides shrugging.

"What can I say? I did it. I went out and lived it up behind my husband's back. What do you want me to plead, temporary nymphomania. The truth is, I did do it, causing untold havoc, and I'm sorry and won't do it again." In a small contrite voice, "Though I can't actually come out and say in all truth that it wasn't sometimes worth it. . . ."

That's the kind of unrepentant wanton I was. . . . Knowing that was the part Rolf wasn't going to forgive, why did I rub it in?

"Oh, yes?" said the doctor, trying to look older, "so this living it up as you call it, was more than just a momentary fancy."

"What do you mean, momentary? . . . She's been running around for damn close to a year."

"I'd hardly call it running around. You make it sound like I've been doling out to telephone repairmen off the trucks."

"You haven't been?"

"Not fair, dammit."

"It's a little late for Robert's rules, don't you think?"

"I think this whole thing is tilting in the wrong direction, if you wanna know what I think."

"In what way?" says the doctor, sympathetic, neutral, understanding, sensitive, probing, insincere, plotting, transparent, pathetic, inevitable. But before I have to make good, the forty-five minutes have gone.

"Well," he says, this presumptuous kid, "see you next Wednesday," and gets up, opens the door, and smiles the same way you smile at funerals, leaving us. Alone? To go home the whole week with no referee? We are both afraid and after leaving, stop for double-dip cones with sprinkles just to create a topic of conversation for the ride.

KATHERINE
June 11

Rolf pretends it never happened. Not Tony. Not the hour. That I didn't say it wasn't sometimes worth it.

KATHERINE
June 14

Tony fades away. Sometimes Chris sits on the floor playing solitaire not exactly right and makes a little moaning sound to herself. Or lies in bed before bed-time and talks singsong the way she used to in her sweet little tone-deaf voice. And I know I didn't really mean that any specific thing was worth it. Or her sudden furious turning on me. Her sudden furious looks. Sparks. Her sudden furious memories, that's not what I mean, that anything was worth that. Only that it separated, not touching either of them, Rolf or Chris . . . that that part was, I can't help it. That part was. Worth a whole lot.

Miranda of the opulent chest and luxuriant hip is back in town again after six months on an ashram in New Mexico. She left New York in a fit of ennui. "It's all so pointless," were her exact words, if I recall correctly. She paid her tuition to the New Mexican lamas with, as they say, "green energy"—to wit, a cool thousand she earned baring her fanny for the photographers of *Oui*. On the ashram she fasted, chanted, meditated, abstained, gathered flowers, assumed the lotus position, and breathed through alternate nostrils. The end result, she told me yesterday (she came up for the night), was a feeling of unbelievable horniness. She sold her return flight ticket and fucked her way home across the Great Plains.

Now this is strange: over the years, Miranda and I must have engaged in a fair score of friendly fucks—after dull parties, when regular lovers were away on business trips, on sweltering New York afternoons. Casual encounters, but torrid screws, every one of them. And last night should have been another. I like Miranda. And what's more, she does have the most cheerful pair of tits ever made. Perky, they are, frolicsome creatures that always seem to be inviting one to come out and play.

But I couldn't play—not "couldn't," "wouldn't." My pecker has developed a mind of its own. And a heart. My pecker has turned into a bloody romantic, lost its *joie de vivre*. My pecker has gone soft on me!

"Hey, that's a new one for you, isn't it, Tony?" grins Miranda.

"It's a sign of my new spirituality," I tell her.

"Want me to give it some help?" she asks.

"Thanks, Miranda, but—"

"Okay, I'll take a rain check."

Wonderful person, Miranda.

"You've got troubles, huh, Tony?"

"Yup," and I tell her, actually the first person I've told it all to. She kissed my head and put me to bed.

What a blessing to have a friend.

KATHERINE
June 15

RETURN TO THE MARRIAGE FIXER.

This time we came in separate cars and sit on separate sides of the waiting room that looks, if possible, tackier than before. I take it all as a personal affront, especially the plastic flowers, gladioli, in a cut plastic vase that looks as if it also has water in it. And he's going to help me? With a self-image from Neisens Five-and-Dime? I look over to share the irritation with Rolf and see the most painful glaze across his eyes. A crisscross of sleepless veins.

"Oh, my poor love," I hear myself murmur, "oh, my poor baby," and come across the room to lay my head in his lap, when the door opens and here we are again. Time to lay out our His and Her versions.

Rolf: I've always been too tied up with my work.

Me: Never been about to postpone immediate gratification.

Rolf: I've let her down.

Me: Substitute gender of personal pronouns.

(INTERCEPTION BY PROFESSIONAL INTERCEPTOR): "Now, now," he says, "Assigning or assuming blame comes to the same thing; why don't we go back to the beginning and tell me what you think actually happened." All Lieutenant Friday wants are the facts.

A fact is a tissue of lies. Rolf told his; me, mine. Yellow Kleenex.

Fact???? Rolf never really for one minute actually believed I meant what I said about I *needed it*? Never? That I was just making it up?

Fact??? That I never really for one minute stopped loving him nevermind how I carried on?

". . . How could you have?" he asked me. He turned and lay all his sleepless nights on my shoulders. Then I don't understand, he said, if you really did love me how could you have done what you did?

And then we said other things. Or the doctor did. I wasn't listening.

I was trying to figure it out myself. Hold Rolf's hand and reassure the two of us at the same time.

Of course I loved him. Love him. That part is beyond questioning. I love Rolf therefore am able to play with myself in the middle of the night in a public telephone booth, am able to spread my legs in a confessional? One thing to question the nature of love in a popular ditty, another to question it.

What could it possibly mean, I love Rolf?

I do not love Rolf.

But I stay with him in spite of the rocks. And don't go off with the love of my life?

Why am I sitting on the end of a vinyl couch in a young man's nylon-covered office instead of sailing off to Byzantium. If I don't love Rolf?

KATHERINE
June 6

Rolf says the fifty bucks isn't worth it. Going to that doctor. I feel quick rushes of adrenalin whenever he mentions quitting. Somehow I don't want to quit, though can't figure out exactly why. What we're getting.

Chris angry in different ways. She said I'm a lousy mother because I don't slice her sandwiches or wrap them in waxed bags like all the other kids' mothers. And don't come to hockey games. Which I do. Assiduously. She doesn't mention THE day, or the day after that one. Her anger is immediate and of short but virulent duration. Her doctor says I must "absorb." I am absorbing. She also assures me a child with a solid foundation in acceptance will not ultimately founder.

I believe her, and think, somewhere in here so does Chris.

ANTONY
June 17

I shall find my pecker neatly enveloped in the cuff of my pajamas some morning, like a dead mouse. Atrophy and natural selection. That is how it was with my ancestors when they awoke one morning and saw their tails lying below their tree like snakes in the grass. Time to clamber down and adapt. My pecker will not die of disuse, it will perish from disappointment. If it cannot slink into Kate, it will slink no more. I will give it a decent burial, as Franco and I did for crashed pigeons and Woolworth turtles. Taps and into the sea with it. Adieu, old friend.

KATHERINE
June 17

Rolf came to bed while I was still up and took me in his arms. He didn't speak. Just held me and petted me while we both stared up into the darkness.

ANTONY
June 18

No more laughing. Time to fall apart again.
What am I waiting for?

KATHERINE
June 25

Chris came home from her hour and at 97 degrees somehow found the strength not only to curse me for three hours but to rip her room apart at the same time. "You bitch" she screamed, loving her power, "You selfish rotten bitch," tearing apart pictures, flinging clothes, hurling books, her doll collection, pillows, old boxes, knitting needles, and the entire collection of childish flotsam she'd built up and refused to part with all these years. "I hate you," she screamed. "I never want to see you again as long as I live," and banging and noise and much nose thumbing and tongue sticking out and feeling better.

"We can't let her talk to you like that," Rolf whispered, anxious to start up the stairs as I held him. "Never mind. I'm just going to have to absorb," crying

172

with both joy and desperation for the final retribution and ultimate dropping of the other shoe.

"I won't," she hollered, ripping up the bedclothes, "and you can't make me." My little girl giving it to me in little girls' terms again. Finally. It's about time. Separating woman from mother, her from me, rage from fear.

"And I don't care if it stays like this for the rest of my life," plopping down in the middle of the mess after I came in to say that now that the storm was over did she want any help putting it all together again?

Sticking her tongue out at me. Letting go a big, smelly fart. But silently grateful when I asked Rolf if he'd give me a hand putting her bed back together. I couldn't handle the headboard and side slats at the same time. Watching—watching!

Whaddya know . . . tempests come, tantrums go, but we're still here.

Did she know where she wanted her Nutshell Series to go?

"Don't you think it's about time we get rid of all these molting robin feathers; it'll give you more room for your rubber-band ball collection?" Until finally she got up, took Ginny Lester's left-handed catcher's mitt to put over there, and then her old Babar books, didn't Daddy know anything? Who puts kid stuff next to C. S. Lewis, anyway? Three hours, the three of us. Throwing out, putting back, cleaning up more than a shambles of a room.

Afterward, we had enough leftovers for a safari to Goodwill and used the one at the Stop & Shop center parking lot, just like that—with no side effects. And then tacos at Bien Venidos.

"Good night, honey," she let me say, if she still wasn't up to an actual kiss. "Good night, honey," with a swipe at her fuzzy yellow hair, and afterward I was crying so hard Rolf had a hard time leaving me for his lair. But he did, even though I was afraid she'd listen.

Know. Feel too powerful? Justified? More confused than ever?

And if it weren't for the smell of the rugula pushing up through the spring earth outside, I'd have lain awake for hours thinking about it.

ANTONY
June 26

I remember one fellow in my Newman Club who insisted that Purgatory must be worse than Hell itself. Though neither of us really believed in either P or H, we passed many an evening arguing the point like the true medieval monks we were probably meant to be.

I finally got his point: If I knew beyond doubt that Kate was lost to me, it would be better than this limbo.

Oh, God, I take it back. I would wait forever.

ANTONY
June 27

I am sinking again.
Somebody help me.

KATHERINE
July 11

"Don't you love Daddy?" Chris said to me while we were clearing off the table.

She said it so softly and so sweetly. It was so unexpected. I was not prepared for such innocence. When she yells at me I think she's meaner than she is. She's not mean at all. She's so little, and it was such an awful thing she had to see, that I didn't even drop the coffee cup, I threw it. Over toward the sink vaguely. . . . "Oh, my baby," folding her into me and crying into her hair. "Yes, my baby, my baby," I told her. "And I love you, too, even though I sometimes yell back."

"You always yell," she said.

"No, I don't," I don't, I don't. Nor do I go out and do bad things to everybody when Daddy turns into an ivory tower without me. Except you don't say everything to little girls. How do you explain the subtle pressures to a small person sorting out beans from lentils? The goods from the bads? I should never have read her *The Five Little Peppers*.

"You can love somebody and still get mad," I can say, but can I? Go into the nature of deprivation. After all, Louisa May Alcott doesn't go into a lot of that.

And even getting mad gets tricky. Cause what about when she gets married and gets mad? Will she end up in a parking lot with her thighs asunder?

I knew I should have thought of this moment before I started.

I will have to absorb more than a sponge. She has. "Do you love Daddy? Do you still love Daddy? What about tomorrow, will you love Daddy, then?"

I've got to remember when she yells at me that sometimes she wants the smell of my hair in hers just the way I still want my mother's, only I can't. And I've got to make sure she can.

"Then why did you do that? . . . You know?" she said to me buried in my blouse.

"Why?"

And she looked up in such confusion and hurt. "Why? Mommy? If you really do love us?"

"Because maybe Daddy didn't love me enough?
Because I'm insatiable?

Because I wanted more (translated we weren't enough for you?)

Because I'm a sex maniac?"

I'm sorry. I suppose I let her down. I didn't know what to say, which is what I said.

"I don't know, honey," I said, afraid of all the other answers. "Sometimes even grown-ups can't put their finger on everything. I really don't know why I did it." I told my little girl a lie because the truth has a lot of porcupine needles, too, you know.

And then I said,

"And I'm so sorry, I wish I could take it all back," when what I really meant was only the part about her barging in on it. The rest? The way I felt then *that I do not feel now,* No, In that heart of hears they write about, No, I'm not sorry, and I suppose, given the golden opportunity again . . . No, not with her in my arms. I won't say it. But I won't promise either.

Through it all, I am still a mess. I still want, and I still don't get.

Settling, as I have settled, for the feel of her arms hugging me. Instead!

KATHERINE
July 16

Today was the first time I was able to walk up and down the aisle of a public shopping center with no one's eye upon me. Mary Magdalene is dead; long live Katherine the Survivor.

. . . And then, there he was! And life did a double take.

I felt my summer rash blossom instantly.

I could feel my palms grip the handlebars of my wagon as I stared down into the pile of Rolf's jelly doughnuts. Tony Amato was staring at me. *The same look as my dream exactly.* Go away, damn you, go away; everything was just getting back to the way it has to be. I couldn't look at him, in spite of my strength, in spite of my steady climb, rung by rung, up the shit pit.

"I am simply not going to just give us up," he is saying to me. He is not what?

Go away from me; my life has just begun cozying itself up again. A couple more pounds on my ravaged flesh and I'd fit into my old bespoke overcoat as good as ever . . . and he's not going to just give us up?

(Subliminal shot of wild dog. Huge, shiny hard-on. Red. As a kid's idealized fire engine.)

I must have cringed. He touched me the way you touch a frightened toddler. "Shhh, lovey," he whispered, "everything's going to be all right," and why was I whimpering, leaning into his touch *as if all this weren't past. Finished. Dead. Quits. All Gone,* no different than Vic Straccusi, or any of the old gang.

"You are destroying me," I whimper.

"Don't you understand what's done is bygone?"

And then the sudden attack of his magnificent obsession. My snake of yore, I can feel him (it—ours??) up through my belly. And a torrential rush of blood through frontal lobes. . . . I rush down aisle C3-4, around D1-2, past a checker reading *Midnight* and then out into the full glare of THE PARKING LOT.

Always the parking lot.

"I don't want this." Shaking with disequilibrium, shaking because the pieces were coming apart again. Itching. Roaring with oceans and tides and seashell noises. "I'm telling you I don't need this!" I'm shouting, and this time there's the feel of his fingers squeezing my shoulders. I know then the memory of his handprint will always be there, gone tomorrow, here today.

"You don't know shit," he's screaming back. "How can you just throw away the best thing in your life?

Tell me," he's bellowing. "Tell me," his fingers growing out of my bones. My shoulders throbbing with splinters.

"Go on, tell me it isn't," he shouts at me. "I dare you. Go on, you stupid bitch, I double-dare you. . . ."

But I can't tell him a bloody thing. Only that the tips of his fingers course with blood and that there's pain through my chest as molten hot as a firebolt from Hephaestus.

"Katey," he's saying, "Katey . . . if it were really finished, would you be shaking? Look at me, baby. Are you going to go all through your life afraid maybe you'll bump into me everytime you go to a supermarket?"

"It is finished. It is finished." I know it's finished. He is talking and I'm intoning. He almost takes me in his arms and I almost let him. I don't want to walk away from him and I don't want to walk back into the store. I have a sudden quite frightening anxiety for the state of my sanity, that maybe I am peeing in my pants.

"Come on," he is saying, pulling on my arm.

People going into the store with wagons and other people coming out. I can feel my temperature dropping in my left leg; it's throbbing with cold. Throbbing. Go away, why did I come here? Where can I go from here? What does the Lord my God want from me; this is worse than Job! I'm not even lucky at cards! Lying in the middle of my life, a sopping sponge with no one to squeeze me out.

Driving is good for the equilibrium. Except you have to remember to turn in a particular direction and steer at the same time which cuts down complete concentration.

On what to do.

The feel of Rolf's hand on my hair. His sweet, sleeping smile against my shoulder. He smells like Cracker Jacks. He doesn't wear underwear. Socks till they reek. *Midnight* magazine when he's depressed. Gets pimples on his ass easily. And chafed elbows. Black. He loves me when he makes love to me.

My daughter must grow up in order to shove off. In good form.

I am also right back where I started whatsis. With an itchy twat, you lying, whorish bitch; what they're saying about you is true. You have a hivey, stinging, ringing, singing, itchy twitching, whatsis when that sonavabitch so much as smells you. You are just as much up that wall as ever. I only hope you don't fall off and crack your skull.

I don't know if he knew I'd come or was hoping, but there were two plates, glasses, everything on the table and the fish already in the oven. Bass, I think, though not sure. Might as well have been beef Wellington for all I tasted of anything. Even though we played an entire three quarters of an hour as if it was as every day as ever.

He asked me for the salt. I passed it.

"The place looks crappy," I said. He said the "gal" who cleaned it quit.

It occurred to me he was needling me. But I didn't dare look up. If I stopped chewing it would all get out of hand, even for a second, one skein of soft belly fish and then another.

He didn't even say, I'm glad you came. Or that his body was throbbing as bad as mine. Neither of us dared look at the other. It was a sort of Churchill Downs obstacle course, eating without knowing, choking on bones or when to swallow.

I am a bad woman, I shall make no more excuses for myself. I have come to this house to taste fish bubbles from this man's mouth. I do not seem to know what it is to feel moral strength, responsibility, or how to mature.

Selfish, my name is Katherine.

And besides the fish bubbles I want every slimy, undigested juice on his tongue.

"Yes," I said, and took off my clothes at his dinner table. "Fuck me, I can't stand it another minute." If I never come again, I don't care, that's not why, not the old "do me" need, "You, you do it better," like playing Mah-Jongg, or bowling three strikes in a row. Just the touch of him. The wet pulse of him on me. I wanted this wop like me, flesh like me, memory like me to lie hard on me and beat me into his body. I wanted him to take me for his purposes. Whatever.

"Tony!" just the sound of his sound . . . ripping off any last shred of fabric. Wanting to rip it. To tear it off me. Get it out of the way. I would bleed my life gone if it wasn't then, all of it, first his tongue knowing how much I'd saved up. His pulling me down so I was a frog. Eating off me, gnawing.

To my bones and beyond, I wanted. Yes, eat off me, it's all I want. I want to grow into your mouth. My feet out of your back. The feel of your grizzled hair and your flinty little body having every piece of skin all at once.

I love you, with his mouth inside my fur piece. Way up inside I could feel him on my ovaries. I love you, with my ass end in his mouth. His body covered mine and would never let me go. I love you, with my legs so tight around his ass he'd be a broken tree trunk, hating him at the same time, pressing him harder. I love you, suck my soreness. Suck me, Tony, I was born for one minute in my life and it was all worth it, feel me harder, feel me more. Feel me, I will smell him to my dying day. I will never wash him off. There is no more time in my space for any other finger squeezing that soft flesh inside my legs, that he pinches till they bruise.

I love you, Tony, I want all and everything there is of you, wet and marking me and having me forever till I'm ashes; you are right, I am a murderer. I will scream with such agony as I flail with this last final orgasm of my life, and from the scream will come other

screams that will never give me another moment's joy,
ever, ever, ever. Make me come so loud I will leave
you deaf. I will pick my rotten pieces up off your floor,
none of them good for anything anymore. Pick up and
run back, coward, into a life that will go on until I'm
ashes, you are right. I am a murderer.

And when this is over I think I can handle the rest.

Fucking is a story in itself. *Nothing to do with love.*
I do not love you, Tony Amato, you go no further than
here. I fuck you, that's what I do. And fuck some
more, more than we shall ever know in our philoso-
phies . . . till I bleed.

Marked with Faulkner's corncob.

Yes, goddamn it, you, Tony, mark me so no man
can ever unsee the scar of you.

*But it isn't life either, you fucking wop. When you're
done, fuck off. I am learning!* Lying dead in each
other's arms, Tristan and Isolde moaning in the background.

Yes, leaving. I wanted to go just as soon as it was
over. As he lay there sure I'd come home never to go
again. As soon as his sleep sank mercilessly into the
pillow, next to my stench. Yes, that's when I wanted to
get the hell out of there.

The Exorcism. The conversion of Saul. DH and
Frieda.

An end to all this. I cannot, do not want to live so
HIGH all the time. It gives me a headache. Much as I
want to fuck you, I want to pull through more. And I
suppose pull Chris with me. Pull my own weight without ending up one around all our necks. And with you,
my Tony, my fuck, I'm an addict. Useless, *And I can't
afford the luxury.*

Dressing in the dark. Tiptoeing out through the
sleep-smelly room. Afraid to go/leave/be found
out/give up. Weak, cowardly, martyred, resolved, com-
promised.

I shall pluck you out of my life, Tony Amato. Next

time you may walk unseen through every supermarket you choose. Want not, waste not . . . like a lot of other people's lives.

And so I reached the door, did not look back, and finally left for good. While he slept thinking I was with him. I am with him. I will be with him.

And then thought better of it, stopped at the phone booth three miles out, and woke him up.

"This isn't life, Tony. People don't fuck in supermarkets. They go there to buy jelly doughnuts for their husbands.

"It's more than I can handle," I said without waiting for his arguments. "I can't do it," a person shouldn't *want* to be marked with a corncob. A person should be thrilled to death to be married to a good screw.

"No," I whispered, crying, when he asked through the silent night if I loved him. And it doesn't really matter where the truth lies.

Somewhere in between is where most of us live anyway.

ANTONY
July 16

There is an end and an ending to the end.

I am leaving on Monday. I am packed.

I had to see her. I could not wait forever. I tracked her, followed her to the supermarket. I begged her. I told her why. And then, finally, I made her feel why. I dug that feeling into her skin, quickly, like a doctor quieting a maniac with a flick of a hypodermic. I scratched the skin for life.

And she came to my house. And we made love in my house. And there is no other lovemaking than the lovemaking Kate and I make together. And it is so much more than anything else, everything else. And it is not enough. It is too much, so it is not enough. And I understand that and I do not. And I am beyond needing to understand that. And so I must leave, quickly.

I lied to Kate for the first time tonight: she thought I was sleeping when she left me. I was not. I was waiting for her to leave.

And later, when she called, I lied again: I said nothing. I did not say I had already packed.

Tonight, when I dug out my passport, I found a note in it I had written to myself three years ago. It said, "Hiyo, Silver!" A little joke from me to me.

I am not sure I can write in this thing any longer.

I am not sure I can do anything any longer.

ANTONY
June 30, 1975
Amsterdam

Dear Mirror, long time no see. Actually, it's been a relief losing touch with myself. My new motto: To thine ownself be evasive.

How do I feel? Zo, zo, as the Dutch say.

The Dutch also say, "Act normal, that's crazy enough." Wonderful people, the Dutch. Tranquilizing. An entire culture built on the philosophy of putting one foot in front of the other. Or in back of the other.

But don't get me wrong, Self, I'm happy as a farkel (Dutch for a pig.) I eat regular and earn my daily bread as an Amsterdam stringer for UPI. Did a big story the other day about the queen's engagement party for her daughter. (She's marrying up . . . a Cuban American.)

And speaking of engagement parties, here I go again. Remember Saskia? Saskia of the serene brow and ample behind? We share a bed and flower vase and

talk of the clomp of little wooden shoes. I am thirty-six
years old. Now or never. And I am tired. Oh, Lord, I
am tired.

I hear occasionally from Edith, Kate's agent—
remember Kate, old friend? We are still collabo-
rating—and the work goes smoother this time with
three thousand miles between us. We're publishing our
diaries—the diaries of our affair—and so between engagement parties for the princess, I scratch through
volume twelve of this thing for the bloody bandages of
my past. How weird it is! Did I really feel that much?
It is only a year and I am reading about a stranger, an
obsessive, destructive stranger. That was not me.
Thank God, that was not me.

Sometimes, late at night while Saskia sleeps, I walk
out and along the canal to where it meets the Amstel
River. I watch the jetsam of Amsterdam flow down
and out to sea.

No, thank God, that was not me.

KATHERINE
July 1, 1975

Ayn Rand invented rape. For me, anyway. That
silent half-desire, half-violation, okay, book rape. Romanticism, I know. I'm not that naive. But tonight,
soaking wet, I swear still slippery, he pressed his hairy
hands against my shoulder, pressed his anger up
against me, and it didn't matter if I was ready or not.

Real. *Fountainhead* romantic, idealized, what every
masochist dreams about book rape, and it was Rolf.
He just didn't give a damn. Whether I came. Whether I
was slippery. He came at me in the hall, mad Rolf Edwards. I know it was from mad. He was giving it to
me, for all the times I gave it away. He whirled me
around and pushed me into the room, slamming it with

his foot. "You're hurting me"—it didn't matter what I told him. He shoved me up against the foot of the bed and kneed my thighs apart just far enough to get it up. Holding me arms apart. Pulling on my breasts as if they had springs instead of nipples. "Stop it, Rolf. . . . Quit it." Only I knew he wouldn't. "Quit it," all the while ready as anything. Hammering at me. Pumping mean. Banging my ass up and back against the brass footboard with the fat, knobby curlicues that kept jabbing into my small, jabbing and hurting and making the whole thing so exciting I came two times to his once. And then he made me get down on the itchy wool rug and worked me and laughed at me till I was crying from exhausted desperation.

"No more . . . no more . . ." I begged him.

"You stupid bitch.

"You ungrateful, dumb, stupid bitch, don't you even know when you're well off?" and then he came again, this time in my mouth.

"What do you think I am, somebody's patsy?" he screamed at me. "You think you can cuckold me in front of that fucking little prick? Don't you know who you're dealing with?" And then shoved this letter from Tony in my face, and left me there throbbing, and sweating, and knowing I'd been had and by whom.

"Goddamn you, Tony," I swore running after him. Not now. I didn't want any intrigue in my life right now. I had all I could hold together right there, going out the door, as I tore out after him in my altogether.

"Where are you going?" Screaming, who cared what the neighbors were in for?

"You can't just leave me, Rolf? . . . Rolf???" To the tune of an exhaust pipe that needed a change of oil and a retreating husband who could play Sheik of Araby with the best of them.

"Rolf? Don't just screw and run," tingly and giddy and knowing he'd probably just gone for a six-pack or a quick one or maybe even a pack of Marlboro's, my rapist. Leaving me with a letter from Tony? Oh, yes, I remember Tony. But then I also remember Esther Agonistes from P.S. one-eighty something.

Postmarked Nederland, Postmarked Prinsengracht 11, postmarked a long time before yesterday. So long I could hardly make out the handwriting. His letter said he was living in Amsterdam; he hoped I was well.